GIANT
PHONICS

T0023599

 This workbook belongs to

....

Dear Parents and Families,

Welcome to the *Giant Phonics* workbook!

The fun activities in this workbook will help improve your child's reading and writing. Your child will also build their pen-control skills and improve their vocabulary. Here are some tips to help ensure they get the most from this book.

- This book is designed to grow with your child. If practical, complete the activities in the order they appear in the book. If an activity is too hard for your child, put it aside until they are ready for it.

- Look at the pages with your child. Each page features a specific sound or group of sounds from the English language. Make sure your child is saying the correct sounds and knows what to do.

- Ensure your child says the words aloud and listens for the featured sound. Phonics is about the relationship between sounds and their spellings. Understanding letter–sound correspondences is key to both reading and writing.

- Read the learning tip on each page before your child starts. It may contain useful information to help you assist your child.

- Make the activity sessions positive experiences. Praise your child's efforts, and point out when progress has been made through practice.

- Encourage your child to take as much time as is needed, rather than rushing. You can help them focus on the current page by pulling it out using the perforations.

- Plan for your child to do only one or two pages a day, and encourage them to look forward to completing another activity on another day.

- There are stickers to use at the back of the book. You can use them as reward stickers, or your child can use them to decorate the pages in any way they like.

We wish your child hours of enjoyment while building their basic reading and writing skills.

Scholastic Early Learning

Picture credits: All photos courtesy of **Shutterstock,** unless noted as follows: **Gargantiopa/Shutterstock.com:** 98tr (motorcycle); **gd_project/Shutterstock. com:** 157tm (Rubik's cube); **Make Believe Ideas:** 13tr (cat), 33ml (lemon), 37mr (nine), 38ml (hen), 38mr (hare), 58ml (rabbit), 101br (kayak), 114bm (lemon), 183tl (troll), 187bl (slime).

Contents

The M Sound

Say the words and listen for the **m sound**. Then trace the **m**'s.

mop

milk

mask

map

moth

man

Make the **m sound**. Then sound out these words.

mom	mat	mud
mug	mix	men

Learning Tip: Show your child how the **m sound** is made with the lips closed. Draw out the sound to make it easy to hear, e.g., *m-m-m-mouse, m-m-m-milk*.

Find the M Sound

Say the word for each picture. Where is the **m sound**?
Draw a line to show whether the **m sound** is at the **start** or **end**.

start

end

Say the sentence. Listen for **m sounds** at the **start**, **middle**, and **end** of words. Then circle the **m**'s.

(M)y mom likes lemons and limes.

Learning Tip: When making the **m sound**, air passes out the nose rather than the mouth. Show this by asking your child to hold their nose and try to make the **m sound**.

Listen for M

Name the **m** foods and listen for the **m sound**.
Put a check by the ones you like.

marsh**m**allows ☐   **m**ushroo**m**s ☐   **m**elon ☐

meatballs ☐   **m**ilkshake ☐   **m**uffin ☐

Say the words and trace the **m**'s.

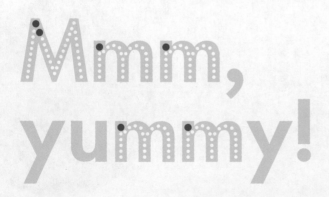

Mmm, yummy!

Learning Tip: List a pair of people or places your child knows, and ask which one starts with the **m sound**. Write the correct answer to show the **M** in place.

Is It the M Sound?

Say each word. Put a check if it **starts** with the **m sound**.
Put an X if it **starts** with a different sound.

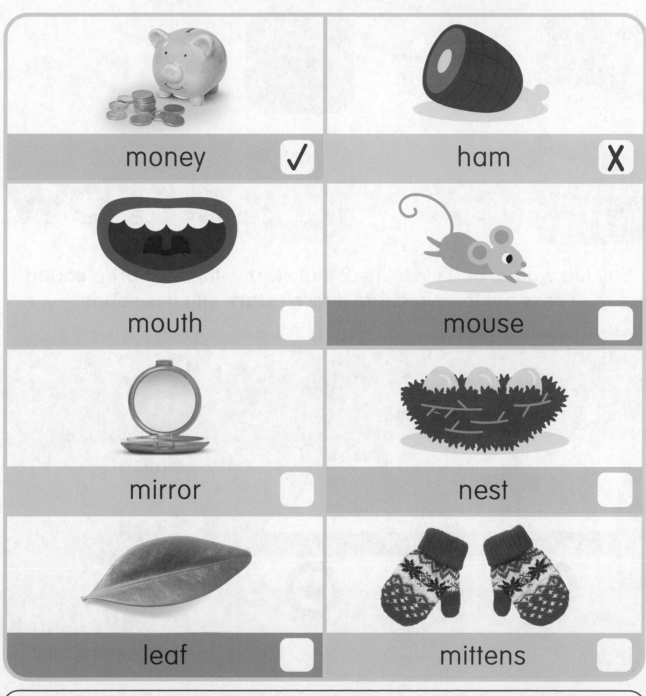

money	✓	ham	X
mouth	☐	mouse	☐
mirror	☐	nest	☐
leaf	☐	mittens	☐

Learning Tip: Show your child that a capital **M** looks a bit like mountain peaks.
Teach them to say *mmm-mountains* while writing **M**'s.

The Short A Sound

Say each word and listen to the **first sound**.
This is the **short a sound**. Then trace the **a**'s.

ant   apple

ax   arrow

Say the words, and circle the 2 that **start** with the **short a sound**.
Cross out the word that doesn't **start** with this sound.

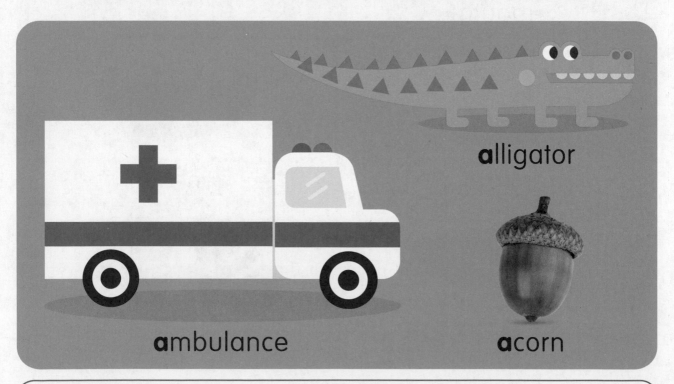

alligator

ambulance   acorn

Learning Tip: In the activity above, *ambulance* and *alligator* start with the **short a sound**, but *acorn* starts with the **long a sound** (the **a** sounds like the letter's name).

Short A in the Middle

Say each word and listen to the **middle sound**.
This is the **short a sound**. Then trace the **a**'s.

cap   bag

sad   can

Say the sentence and listen for 5 **short a sounds**.
Circle them in the sentence.

Sam and Dad had a nap.

Learning Tip: The word *a* does not usually have the short or long a sound. Instead, it has the **uh (schwa) sound**. See pages 204–205 for more on this sound.

Write Short A

Say each word and listen for the **short a sound**. Then trace the **a**'s.

fan   rat   flag

Write the missing **a** in each word. Then say the word
and listen for the **short a sound**.

m_n

p_n

c_t

b_t

t_g

h_nd

Learning Tip: Encourage your child to sound out each word above and listen for the
short a sound. Help with any letter sounds that your child doesn't know.

Short A Puzzle

Say the words. Color the parts with **short a sound words red**.
Color the parts with other words green. What word with the
short a sound is in the picture?

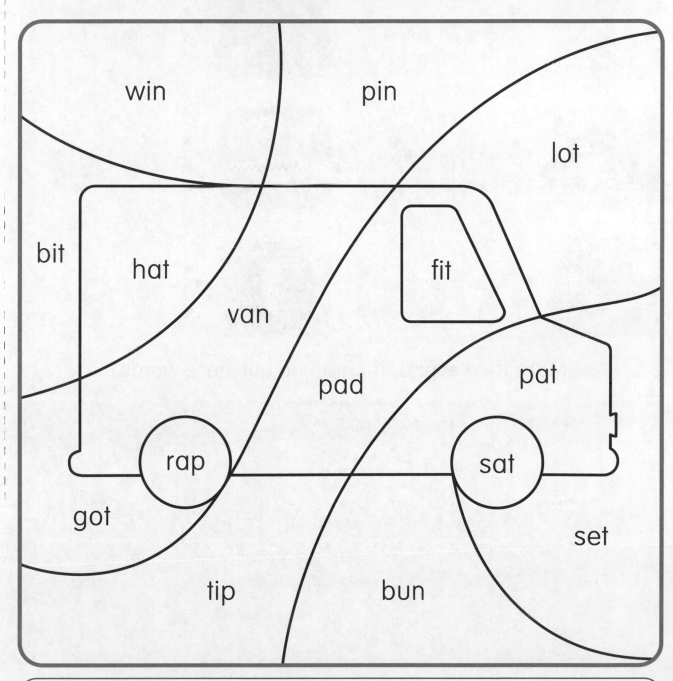

win

pin

lot

bit

hat

fit

van

pad

pat

rap

sat

got

set

tip

bun

Learning Tip: Ask your child to place a hand under their chin while saying the
short a sound words. Help them notice their chin go down a little to make this sound.

The T Sound

Say the words and listen for the **t sound**. Then trace the **t**'s.

tie

top

tent

taxi

toad

tire

Make the **t sound**. Then sound out these words.

tan	ten	tot
tap	tug	tip

Learning Tip: Consonant-vowel-consonant (CVC) words have a short vowel in the middle and are simple, easy-to-blend first words to read.

Find the T Sound

Say the word for each picture. Where is the **t sound**?
Draw a line to show whether the **t sound** is at the **start** or **end**.

start

end

Say the sentence. Listen for **t sounds** at the **start**, **middle**, and **end** of words. Then circle the **t**'s.

Toby waters a pretty plant.

> **Learning Tip:** In the word *truck*, the **t** is followed by another consonant. It forms the blend **tr**. If necessary, help your child hear the **t sound** at the start of this word.

T at the Start

Say the word for each picture. If it **starts** with the **t sound**, draw a line from the picture to the **t**'s.

Learning Tip: Using magnetic letters, spell out a different word on your fridge door each night. Have fun helping your child sound it out in the morning.

Count T Sounds

Say each word. How many times do you hear the **t sound**?
Circle the number.

tomato	1 ②

turtle	1 2

truck	1 2

tutu	1 2

tiptoes	1 2

trees	1 2

ADMIT ONE	
ticket	1 2

tail	1 2

Learning Tip: Provide chances to practice the learning. For example, point to the tomatoes in your child's dinner and say, "What sound does this food start with?"

The S Sound

Say the words and listen for the **s sound**. Then trace the **s**'s.

sun

saw

sing

sub

sad

star

Make the **s sound**. Then sound out these words.

sob	set	sit
sum	sat	sip

Learning Tip: To help your child hear the **s sound**, say something like, "S-s-s-sneaky s-s-s-snakes go *hiss-s-s-s, hiss-s-s-s, hiss-s-s-s.*" Encourage your child to join in.

Find the S Sound

Say the word for each picture. Where is the **s sound**?
Draw a line to show whether the **s sound** is at the **start** or **end**.

start

end

Say the sentence. Listen for **s sounds** at the **start**, **middle**, and **end** of words. Then circle the **s**'s.

Six sassy snakes sing a silly song.

Learning Tip: When your child is first learning the **s sound**, avoid teaching **s** words that have the **sh sound**, such as *sugar* and *shoes*, or the **z sound**, such as *is* and *music*.

Listen for S

Read the words aloud and listen for the **s sound**.
Then draw lines to match the words to the pictures.

six

kiss

sip

yes

sand

books

6

Learning Tip: We often make the plural of a word by adding the **s sound** to the end (e.g., *cat* and *cats*), but sometimes we use the **z sound** (e.g., *tree* and *trees*).

C and the S Sound

Say the words and listen for the **s sound**. Then trace the **c**'s that stand for the **s sound**. Draw lines to match the words to the pictures.

city

cereal

cents

celery

circus

circle

> **Learning Tip:** Note that the first **c** in *circus* and *circle* stands for the **s sound**, but the second **c** stands for the **k sound**.

The P Sound

Say the words and listen for the **p sound**. Then trace the **p's**.

pear

paw

peas

pie

pig

pink

Make the **p sound**. Then sound out these words.

pan	pen	pip
pot	pup	pin

Learning Tip: The **p sound** is not vocalized. Close the lips with the teeth apart, then open the lips with a puff of air. Avoid saying *puh*. We say *p-en* not *puh-en*.

Find the P Sound

Say the word for each picture. Where is the **p sound**?
Draw a line to show whether the **p sound** is at the **start** or **end**.

start

end

Say the sentence. Listen for **p sounds** at the **start**, **middle**,
and **end** of words. Then circle the **p**'s.

Pippa's pony goes clip, clop.

Learning Tip: Together, practice saying the **p sound** in front of **p** words.
For example, say *p-p-p-pie* or *p-p-p-pony*.

P in the Middle

Say the word for each picture.
Circle the word if you hear the **p sound** in the middle.

zipper

slippers

(hippo)

ribbon

happy

spy

apple

butter

sunny

puppet

Learning Tip: When sounding out words, children often leave out middle sounds. Activities such as this help them pay attention to all the sounds in a word.

Lots of P Sounds

Say the words and listen for **p sounds**.
Then circle the **p**'s in the words.

popcorn

pumpkin

puppy

pepper

Read the sentence and listen for **p sounds**.
Then circle the **p**'s, and color the Popsicle.

Piper has a
purple Popsicle.

Learning Tip: You could practice the **p sound** in a fun way by teaching your child this tongue twister: Peter Piper picked a peck of pickled peppers.

CVC Words

Sound out the words.
Then draw lines to match the words to the pictures.

map

pat

sat

mat

tap

Sam

Learning Tip: These consonant-vowel-consonant (CVC) words practice the sounds covered by the activities so far.

A is for Animal

Name each animal and listen to the **first sound**. Then draw a line to match the picture to the letter that stands for that sound.

m

s

t

p

a

Learning Tip: The beginning sounds (or initial sounds) on this page are among some of the easiest sounds for children to hear and learn.

The Short I Sound

Say each word and listen to the **first sound**.
This is the **short i sound**. Then trace the **i**'s.

in

insect

ill

itch

Say the words, and circle the 2 that **start** with the **short i sound**.
Cross out the word that doesn't **start** with this sound.

iron

inside

igloo

Learning Tip: In the activity above, *inside* and *igloo* start with the **short i sound**, but *iron* starts with the **long i sound** (the **i** sounds like the letter's name).

26

Short I in the Middle

Say each word and listen to the **middle sound**.
This is the **short i sound**. Then trace the **i**'s.

6 six

rip

bib

sit

Say the sentence and listen for 5 **short i sounds**.
Circle them in the sentence.

A pink pig gives Tim a gift.

Learning Tip: Draw your child's attention to small high-frequency words with the **short i sound** (such as *is*, *if*, *it*, and *in*) in books and on signs. Ask your child to read them.

Write Short I

Say each word and listen for the **short i sound**. Then trace the **i**'s.

 **dig**

 **hit**

 **wig**

Write the missing **i** in each word.
Then say the word and listen for the **short i sound**.

l_d

l_ps

f_n

m_lk

p_n

sh_p

> **Learning Tip:** The **short i sound** occurs often but can be missed in children's spelling. Teach them that all words have a vowel and to listen carefully to figure out which to use.

Short I Puzzle

Say each word and listen for the **short i sound**.
Then find and circle it in the word search.

fish   **kick**   **swim**   **drink**   **did**   **win**

s	m	a	p	c	d	s	w	i	m
q	f	d	t	w	s	i	o	n	d
u	i	v	l	k	m	o	r	p	t
i	s	n	g	w	i	n	i	a	b
o	h	a	i	g	q	z	d	y	n
q	i	k	c	h	d	l	p	u	q
s	f	m	l	u	r	s	i	q	z
h	n	y	k	i	i	e	d	i	d
i	g	a	t	d	n	r	a	d	e
r	w	k	i	c	k	q	x	b	c

Learning Tip: To keep a focus on phonics, ensure your child says each word and listens for the **short i sound** before finding it in the word search.

The D Sound

Say the words and listen for the **d sound**. Then trace the **d**'s.

dog

deer

desk

doll

duck

door

Make the **d sound**. Then sound out these words.

dot	dad	den
dig	dug	dip

Learning Tip: If your child confuses the **b** and **d sounds**, say *bed* and discuss how the **b sound** starts with a shut mouth and the **d sound** starts with an open mouth.

Find the D Sound

Say the word for each picture. Where is the **d sound**?
Draw a line to show whether the **d sound** is at the **start** or **end**.

start

end

Say the sentence. Listen for **d sounds** at the **start**
and in the **middle** of words. Then circle the **d's**.

Dad's dog dives in a muddy puddle.

Learning Tip: Have fun practicing the **d sound** with your child by writing
and repeating simple syllables such as *da, da, da* or *do, do, do*.

Listen for D

In each row, say the first word and listen for the **d sound**. Then name the other pictures. Color the one that **starts** with the **d sound**.

In each row, say the first word and listen for the **d sound**. Then name the other pictures. Color the one that **ends** with the **d sound**.

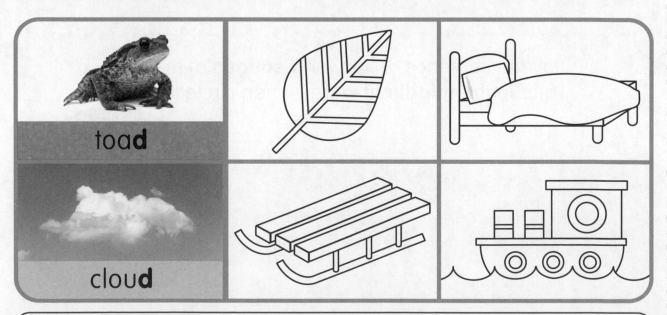

Learning Tip: Write a list of familiar actions that contain the **d sound**, such as *dig*, *dip*, and *dive*. Make the actions with your child as they practice sounding out each word.

Follow the D Sound

Say the words. Then join up the ones with the **d sound** in the **middle** to help Eddy to the finish.

start ➡

Eddy	radio	pumpkin	mittens	lion
plant	ladder	balloon	guitar	rabbit
lemon	puddle	candy	soda	medal
spoon	book	astronaut	jewel	**finish** teddy

Learning Tip: Help your child understand that when the letter **d** is doubled in words such as *ladder* and *puddle*, one of the **d**'s is silent (see page 240).

The N Sound

Say the words and listen for the **n sound**. Then trace the **n**'s.

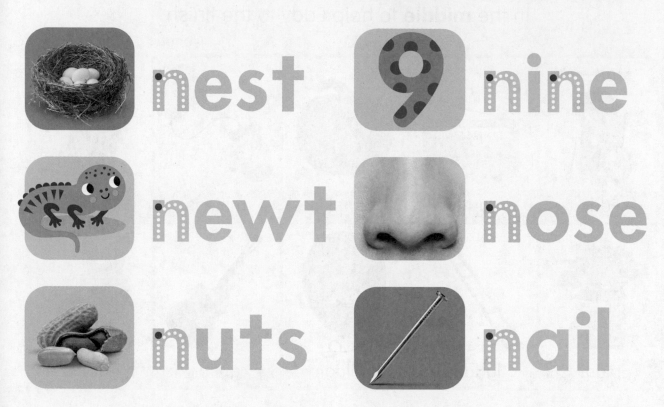

nest   nine

newt   nose

nuts   nail

Make the **n sound**. Then sound out these words.

nod	nib	net
nap	nub	not

Learning Tip: Ask your child to guess your instruction by listening to the beginning sound. E.g., say, "Put your finger on your n-n-n…" Pause for them to say *nose*.

Find the N Sound

Say the word for each picture. Where is the **n sound**?
Draw a line to show whether the **n sound** is at the **start** or **end**.

start

end

Say the sentence. Listen for **n sounds** at the **start**, **middle**, and **end** of words. Then circle the **n**'s.

Nan ate nine green beans.

Learning Tip: Some pictures in this book don't have labels. This is so the child has to say the words and listen to the sounds rather than match letter shapes.

Is It the N Sound?

Say each word. Put a check if it **starts** with the **n sound**.
Put an X if it **starts** with a different sound.

net ☐   dragon ☐

octopus ☐   nap ☐

nachos ☐   robot ☐

panda ☐   numbers ☐

Learning Tip: If your child struggles with decoding words, model this for them.
E.g., say, "Do you want to take a n-a-p?"

Is It N or M?

Say the word for each picture. Circle the correct letter to show if it **starts** with the **n sound** or the **m sound**.

N (M)

N M

N M

N M

N M

N M

> **Learning Tip:** Children often confuse the **n** and **m sounds**. Use the words on this page to practice listening to the difference between the two sounds.

The H Sound

Say the words and listen for the **h sound**. Then trace the **h**'s.

hill

hose

hen

hat

horn

hare

Make the **h sound**. Then sound out these words.

ham	hut	hem
hog	hip	hop

Learning Tip: Show your child how your breath fogs a mirror when saying the **h sound**. This will help them understand that we push our breath out to make the sound.

Find the H Sound

Say the word for each picture. Does it **start** with the **h sound**?
Draw a line from the words that **start** with the **h sound** to the **h**'s.

Say the sentence. Listen for **h sounds**.
Then circle the **h**'s.

Harry's horse hates hay.

Learning Tip: Vocalizing exaggerated laugh sounds such as *ho, ho, ho* and *mwa-ha-ha-ha* is a fun way to practice the **h sound**.

Hunt for H

Color **H**azel the **h**appy **h**edgehog. Then name and circle 5 other things in the picture that **start** with the **h sound**.

Hazel the happy hedgehog

Learning Tip: Choose a letter sound to focus on during a long car journey. Ask your child to find things that begin with that sound as they look out the window.

Hop for H

Sound out the words. Then draw a line linking the words that **start** with the **h sound** to help **H**annah finish the **h**opscotch.

start → hot

hiss

hen | dig

him

mop | hop

ham

hug | nap

hat → finish

Learning Tip: Phonics hopscotch is a fun game. Draw a hopscotch grid in washable chalk, and ask your child to hop on all the words that start with a specific sound.

Word Scramble

Say the word for each picture. Then trace the lines to help you write the correct letter in each space.

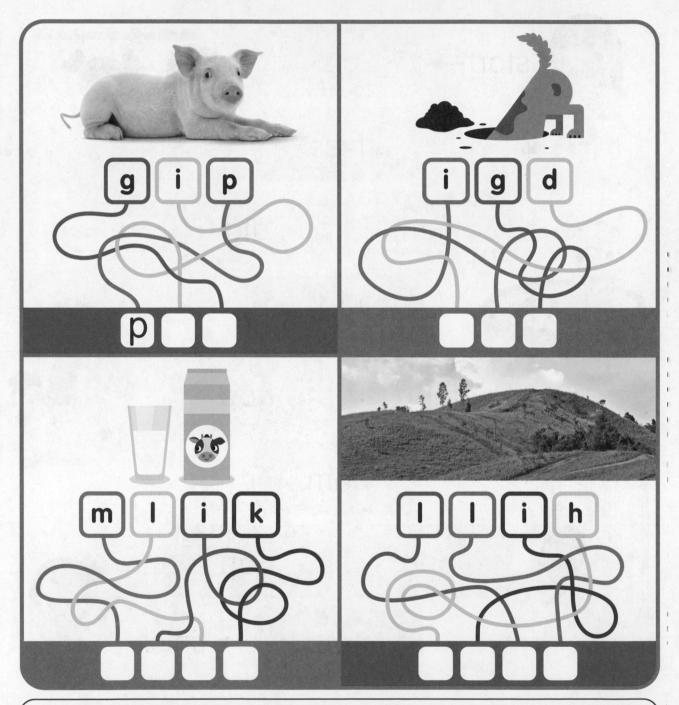

Learning Tip: Introduce further practice by making deliberate mistakes with letter sounds when reading words aloud. Encourage your child to correct you.

Color the Letters

Say the words and listen to their **first** and **last** sounds.
Then use the key to color the letters.

Key: i = purple, d = orange, n = green, h = red, t = blue, s = pink

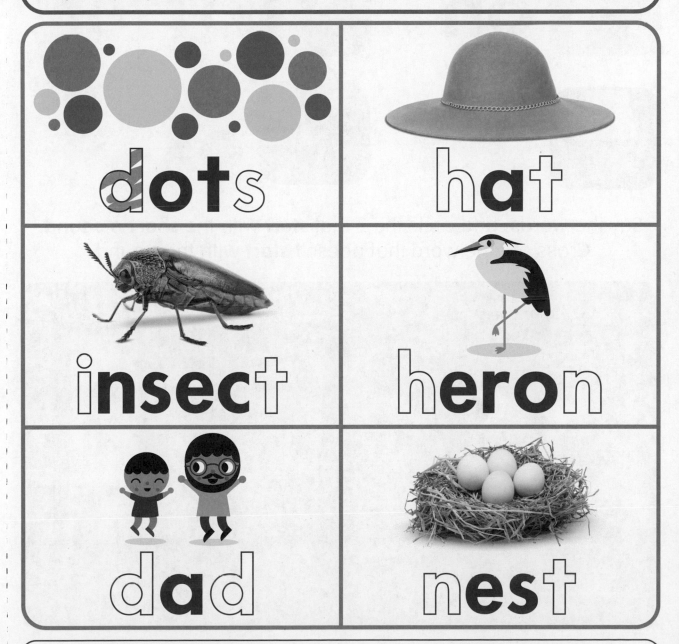

dots

hat

insect

heron

dad

nest

Learning Tip: Your child might need to say each word a few times, focusing on identifying the first sound and then the last sound.

The Short O Sound

Say each word and listen to the **first sound**.
This is the **short o sound**. Then trace the **o**'s.

on   otter

off   ox

Say the words, and circle the 2 that **start** with the **short o sound**.
Cross out the word that doesn't **start** with this sound.

octopus   orange   open

Learning Tip: In the activity above, *octopus* and *orange* start with the **short o sound**,
but *open* starts with the **long o sound** (the **o** sounds like the letter's name).

Short O in the Middle

Say each word and listen to the **middle sound**.
This is the **short o sound**. Then trace the **o**'s.

pop

dog

fox

hot

Say the sentence and listen for 4 **short o sounds**.
Circle them in the sentence.

A frog hops on a log.

Learning Tip: Say the **short o sound** with your child to help them notice the round o-shape of the mouth.

45

Write Short O

Say each word and listen for the **short o sound**. Then trace the **o**'s.

jog   top   sob

Write the missing **o** in each word.
Then say the word and listen for the **short o sound**.

m_m   kn_t

l_ck   s_ck

b_x   STOP st_p

Learning Tip: When traveling, ask your child to sound out simple words on signs, such as *STOP* or *Coffee Shop*.

Short O Puzzles

Say the words below and listen for the **short o sound**.
Then use the words and picture clues to finish the puzzles.

hop) (log) (dog) (fox) (top) (hog) (pot) (mop

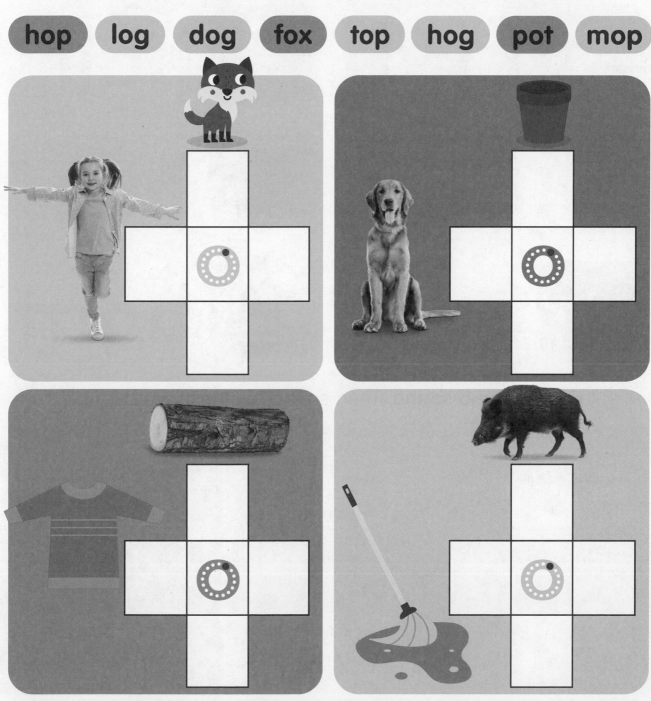

Learning Tip: If your child or someone your child knows has a name with a **short o sound** (e.g., *Tom*, *Olive*, *Oscar*, *Molly*), write it down and discuss the sound together.

47

The B Sound

Say the words and listen for the **b sound**. Then trace the **b**'s.

bird

ball

bag

bug

bear

boat

Make the **b sound**. Then sound out these words.

bat	bed	bit
bop	bun	bus

Learning Tip: Ask your child to put a hand in front of their lips and to make the **b sound**. Help them notice a small puff of air hit their hand as they make the sound.

Find the B Sound

Say the word for each picture. Where is the **b sound**?
Draw a line to show whether the **b sound** is at the **start** or **end**.

start

end

Say the sentence. Listen for **b sounds** at the **start**, **middle**, and **end** of words. Then circle the **b**'s.

A baby bear is a cub.

Learning Tip: Make a short, fast sound to demonstrate the **b sound**. Avoid saying *buh* because it sounds wrong when blending: we say *b-ee*, not *buh-ee*.

B is for Birthday

Say the names and circle all the **b sounds** you hear.
Then use the 3 clues to figure out who is having a **b**irthday.
Check the correct person.

Ben ☐　　Jacob ☐　　Betty ☐

Caleb ☐　　Bobby ☐　　Beth ☐

Clue 1	Clue 2	Clue 3
blue bow tie	brown boots	big badge

Learning Tip: Ask your child to practice letter sounds by thinking of alliterative names for people in your family, such as *Brilliant Brother* or *Magical Mommy*.

Listen for B

Say each word. How many times do you hear the **b sound**?
Circle the number.

baboon 1 2   zebra 1 2

baby 1 2   bee 1 2

Say the word for each picture.
Circle the word if you hear the **b sound** anywhere.

rabbit   kitten   button   bubbles

Learning Tip: Take this opportunity to practice the **t sound** by asking your child what sound they heard in the middle of *kitten* and *button*.

The R Sound

Say the words and listen for the **r sound**. Then trace the **r**'s.

rat

rug

run

rose

ring

ruby

Make the **r sound**. Then sound out these words.

rot	rip	red
rag	rub	ram

Learning Tip: Many children do not develop the ability to make the **r sound** until they are six or seven, so be patient with your child if they find this difficult.

Find the R Sound

Say the word for each picture. Where is the **r sound**?
Draw a line to show whether the **r sound** is at the **start** or **end**.

start

end

Say the sentence. Listen for **r sounds** at the **start**, **middle**,
and **end** of words. Then circle the **r**'s.

Roger has a red and green parrot.

Learning Tip: Children often substitute the **w sound** for the **r sound**. Practice the
sounds using word pairs where only the first sound differs (e.g., *rail/wail, ring/wing*).

R at the Start

Say the word for each picture. If it **starts** with the **r sound**,
draw a line from the picture to the **r**'s.

Rr

Learning Tip: You could help your child practice the **r sound** by singing
the nursery rhyme *Row, Row, Row Your Boat* together.

Is It the R Sound?

Make each animal sound. Check the ones that contain the **r sound**.

Moo! ☐

Roar! ☐

Meow! ☐

Ribbit! ☐

Growl! ☐

Baa! ☐

Learning Tip: Encourage your child to listen to the sounds in their environment by asking them questions such as, "What sound does that bird make?"

The L Sound

Say the words and listen for the **l sound**. Then trace the **l**'s.

log

lips

lion

leaf

lime

lake

Make the **l sound**. Then sound out these words.

leg	lap	lid
lug	lot	lob

Learning Tip: To sound out CVC words, tap once for each sound along your arm. Then say the whole word as you slide your hand down your arm. Ask your child to copy you.

Find the L Sound

Say the word for each picture. Where is the **l sound**?
Draw a line to show whether the **l sound** is at the **start** or **end**.

start

end

Say the sentence. Listen for **l sounds** at the **start**, **middle**, and **end** of words. Then circle the **l**'s.

Laurel licks a large lollipop.

Learning Tip: Practice **l sounds** by offering sentence prompts. E.g., say, "Lucy loves learning about …," and ask your child to fill in the blank.

L in the Middle

Say the word for each picture.
Circle the word if you hear the **l sound** in the **middle**.

gorilla

melon

shelf

carrot

rabbit

pillow

lollipop

dolphin

button

umbrella

Learning Tip: The letter **l** on its own usually stands for the **l sound**. However, other spellings for the **l sound** include *castle* and *muscle*.

Link the L Sounds

Say the words, and join up the ones with the **l sound** at the **start**, **middle**, or **end** to help Lucy reach the finish.

start →				
Lucy	lily	hippo	hat	dress
dinosaur	lobster	popcorn	snake	tractor
rocket	ruler	lamp	panda	muffin
pudding	mermaid	ball	ladybug	**finish** piglet

Learning Tip: For extra practice, ask your child to tell you if the **l sounds** in each word are at the start, in the middle, or at the end.

The G Sound

Say the words and listen for the **g sound**. Then trace the **g**'s.

gift girl

golf gull

goat gate

Make the **g sound**. Then sound out these words.

gap	get	gig
gas	got	gum

Learning Tip: This **g sound** is sometimes called the **hard g sound**. It is most commonly heard in front of the letters **a**, **o**, and **u** (e.g., *gas*, *got*, and *gum*).

Find the G Sound

Say the word for each picture. Where is the **g sound**?
Draw a line to show whether the **g sound** is at the **start** or **end**.

start

end

Say the sentence. Listen for **g sounds** at the **start**, **middle**, and **end** of words. Then circle the **g**'s.

Greg got some good goggles.

Learning Tip: If your child struggles with the **g sound**, ask them to lie on their back and say it. Their tongue will fall to the back of their mouth, making the **g sound** easier.

Listen for G

In each row, say the first word and listen for the **g sound**. Then name the other pictures. Color the one that **starts** with the **g sound**.

In each row, say the first word and listen for the **g sound**. Then name the other pictures. Color the one that **ends** with the **g sound**.

Learning Tip: Praise your child when they self-monitor their reading. They will learn more quickly if they can notice and correct their own mistakes.

Lots of G Sounds

Say the words and listen for the **g sounds**.
Then count the **g sounds** in each word, and draw a line
from the word to the number.

bug

tiger

gigg**l**e

1

2

di**gg**er

yo**g**urt

go**gg**les

Learning Tip: The words *giggle*, *goggles*, and *digger* have **double g's** in the middle.
However, the **double g's** stand for only one **g sound** (see pages 240–243).

The J Sound

Say the words and listen for the **j sound**. Then trace the **j**'s.

jet

jar

jay

joy

jam

jaw

Make the **j sound**. Then sound out these words.

jig	jot	jog
job	jab	jut

Learning Tip: After practicing the words on this page, ask your child to name other words they know that start with the **j sound**. Give helpful hints if necessary.

Find the J Sound

Say the word for each picture. Does it **start** with the **j sound**?
Draw a line from the words that **start** with the **j sound** to the **j**'s.

Say the sentence. Listen for **j sounds** at the **start**
and in the **middle** of words. Then circle the **j**'s.

Jojo the jaguar plays the banjo.

Learning Tip: If your child struggles to read multisyllable words, cover up part of
a word with your hand and ask them to sound it out one syllable at a time.

G and the J Sound

Say the words and listen for the **j sound**. Then trace the **g**'s that stand for the **j sound**. Lastly, match the words to the pictures.

gem

giant

magic

giraffe

orange

cabbage

Learning Tip: When the letter **g** stands for the **j sound** (as in *gem* and *giraffe*), teachers sometimes refer to it as having the **soft g sound**.

G in a Sentence

Say the sentence and listen for **j sounds**. Then circle 6 **g**'s that stand for the **j sound**, and finish coloring the picture.

The giant, orange giraffe ate magic gingerbread.

Learning Tip: The letter **g** usually stands for the **j sound** if it is before **e**, **i**, or **y** (*gem*, *giant*, *gym*). However, a **double g** usually stands for the **g sound**.

Short O Search

Say the word for each picture and listen for the **short o sound**.
Then find and circle the words in the word search.

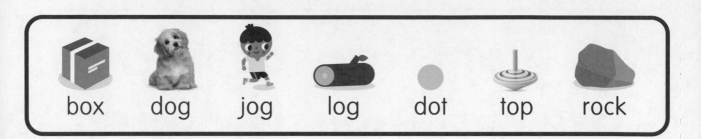

box   dog   jog   log   dot   top   rock

h	o	v	e	a	c	v	i
i	p	l	q	d	b	o	x
f	z	r	h	q	m	k	g
p	a	o	d	k	g	j	u
e	h	c	j	r	b	o	s
d	n	k	n	l	o	g	s
o	e	i	f	b	c	h	t
t	o	p	y	w	d	o	g

Learning Tip: This page gives your child the opportunity to practice the **short o sound** in combination with some of the consonant sounds they have learned so far.

At the Beach

Say the words for the pictures. Then write the letters that stand for the missing sounds to finish labeling the scene.

__ighthouse

__ock

__et

__ull

__irl

__obster

__all

__ucket

Learning Tip: Use pictures to practice letter sounds. Pictures are useful visual cues for children as they can focus on sounds without having to read the word.

The Short E Sound

Say each word and listen to the **first sound**.
This is the **short e sound**. Then trace the **e**'s.

egg

elf

elk

exit

Say the words, and circle the 2 that **start** with the **short e sound**.
Cross out the word that doesn't **start** with this sound.

eagle

elbow

elephant

Learning Tip: In the activity above, *elbow* and *elephant* start with the **short e sound**, but *eagle* starts with the **long e sound** (the e sounds like the letter's name).

Short E in the Middle

Say each word and listen to the **middle sound**.
This is the **short e sound**. Then trace the **e**'s.

bed   gem

jet   hen

Say the sentence and listen for 5 **short e sounds**.
Circle them in the sentence.

Emma fed ten red hens.

Learning Tip: Using a mirror, show your child how their mouth forms a smile
and their chin drops slightly when they make the **short e sound**.

Write Short E

Say each word and listen for the **short e sound**. Then trace the **e**'s.

net pen vet

Write the missing **e** in each word.
Then say the word and listen for the **short e sound**.

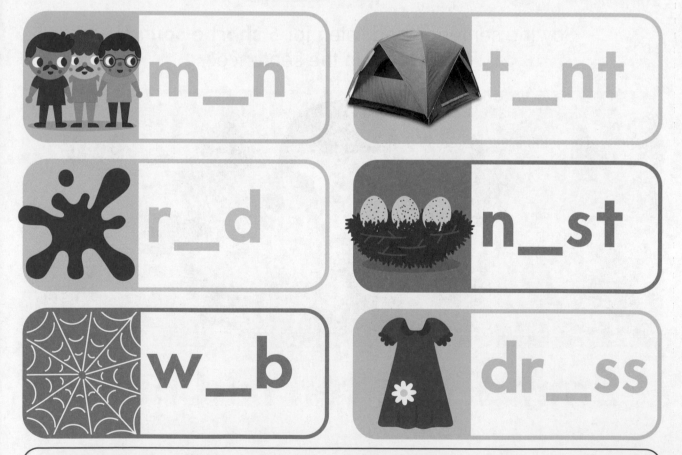

m_n t_nt

r_d n_st

w_b dr_ss

Learning Tip: Children often confuse the **short e** and **short i** sounds. Compare pairs such as *ten*/*tin* or *mess*/*miss*, and help your child notice the different mouth shapes.

Short E Puzzle

Say the words. Color the parts with **short e sound words orange**. Color the parts with **other words blue**. What word with the **short e sound** is in the picture?

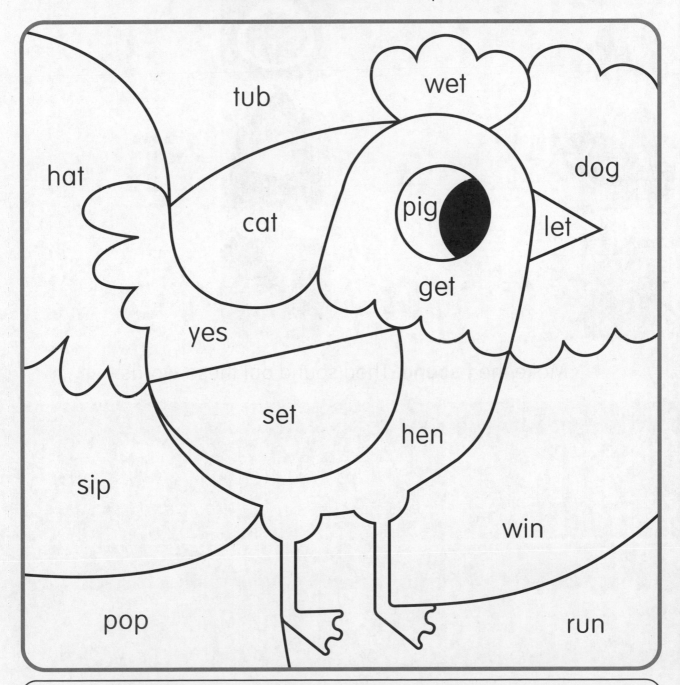

Learning Tip: To practice the other short vowel sounds, discuss the vowel sound in each word as your child completes the puzzle.

The F Sound

Say the words and listen for the **f sound**. Then trace the **f**'s.

fox

fig

fish

fire

fern

fork

Make the **f sound**. Then sound out these words.

fin	fog	fit
fan	fun	fed

Learning Tip: Say the letter sounds in a CVC word, and ask your child to blend them into a word. E.g., if you say *f-a-n*, your child should answer *fan*.

Find the F Sound

Say the word for each picture. Where is the **f sound**?
Draw a line to show whether the **f sound** is at the **start** or **end**.

start

end

Say the sentence. Listen for **f sounds** at the **start**, **middle**, and **end** of words. Then circle the **f**'s.

Fifi the fairy flew off to Fiji.

TO FIJI

Learning Tip: To make the **f sound**, rest your front teeth on your bottom lip and blow out your breath. Use a mirror so your child can see where to place their teeth.

Fish for F

Sound out the words. Then draw a line from each fishing rod to a word that **starts** with the **f sound**.

Learning Tip: Read a story that focuses on the **f sound**, such as *One Fish, Two Fish, Red Fish, Blue Fish* by Dr. Seuss. Ask your child to listen for the **f sound**.

Where Is the F?

Say the word for each picture. Check the box that matches where you hear the **f sound**. There is one box for each sound in the word.

Learning Tip: Adapt this activity to practice other sounds. Draw linked boxes. Ask your child to listen for a specific sound in a word and put a counter in the correct box.

The K Sound

Say the words and listen for the **k sound**. Then trace the **k**'s.

kid

key

king

kite

Say the word for each picture. Where is the **k sound**?
Draw a line to show whether the **k sound** is at the **start** or **end**.

start

end

Learning Tip: The letter **k** stands for the **k sound** when it is followed by a **vowel**, but it is silent when followed by an **n** (see page 174).

K at the Start

Say the word for each picture. If it **starts** with the **k sound**, draw a line from the picture to the **k**'s.

Kk

Learning Tip: Say a set of three words and ask your child to tell you which **first** sound they have in common. This activity can also be used to practice **middle** and **end** sounds.

CK and the K Sound

Say the words and listen for the **k sound**. Then trace the **ck**'s.

kick

sock

lock

neck

clock

duck

Say the sentence. Listen for **k sounds** in the **middle** and at the **end** of words. Then circle the **ck**'s.

Jack and Mick snack on a pack of pickles.

Learning Tip: Help your child understand that the letters **ck** are used to spell the **k sound** when the sound follows a **short vowel sound**.

Lots of K Sounds

Say the rhyme and listen for the **k sounds**.
Then circle the **ck**'s, and finish coloring the picture.

Hickory, dickory, dock,
the mouse ran up the clock.
The clock struck one,
the mouse ran down.
Hickory, dickory, dock!

Learning Tip: As well as practicing the **k sound**, this nursery rhyme provides an opportunity for children to review the **h**, **d**, and **m sounds**.

C and the K Sound

Say the words and listen for the **k sound**.
Then trace the **c**'s that stand for the **k sound**.

car

cod

cat

cow

coat

cake

Make the **k sound**. Then sound out these words.

cap	cog	cub
cot	cup	can

Learning Tip: The letter **c** usually stands for the **k sound** when it is followed by an **a**, **o**, or **u**, as in the words *can*, *cot*, and *cub*.

Find the K Sound

Say the word for each picture. Does it **start** with the **k sound**?
Draw a line from the words that **start** with the **k sound** to the **c**'s.

Say the sentence. Listen for **k sounds** at the **start**
and in the **middle** of words. Then circle the **c**'s.

Cara eats a coconut cupcake.

Learning Tip: Point out to your child that they will also hear a **k sound** at the **end**
of the word *cupcake*, but in this case it is spelled with the letter **k**.

83

Search for C

Color **C**arlos the **c**ool **c**at. Then find and circle 4 other things in the picture that **start** with the **k sound**.

Carlos the cool cat

Learning Tip: The letter **c** usually stands for the **k sound** when it is followed by a consonant, as in the words *cloud* and *crab*.

Is It the K Sound?

Say each word. Put a check if it **starts** with the **k sound**.
Put an X if it **starts** with a different sound.

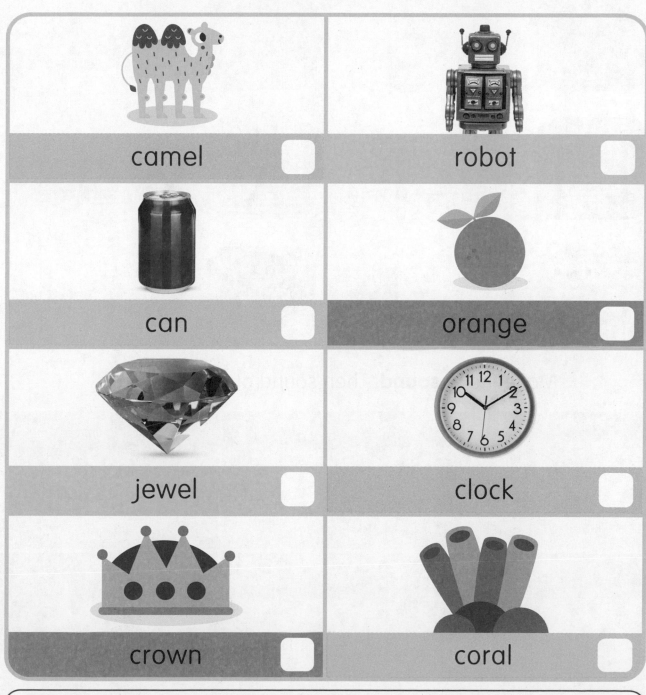

camel	robot
can	orange
jewel	clock
crown	coral

Learning Tip: Remind your child that the letter **c** can stand for more than one sound.
Write and say some **c** words, and ask your child if they hear the **s** or the **k sound**.

The W Sound

Say the words and listen for the **w sound**. Then trace the **w**'s.

wig   web

well   wax

wolf   wink

Make the **w sound**. Then sound out these words.

wet	win	wit
wag	wed	wok

Learning Tip: Ask your child to clap once for each separate sound as they sound out the CVC words on this page. This will help them identify individual sounds.

Find the W Sound

Say the word for each picture. Does it **start** with the **w sound**?
Draw a line from the words that **start** with the **w sound** to the **w**'s.

Say the sentence. Listen for **w sounds** at the **start**
and in the **middle** of words. Then circle the **w**'s.

We always want kiwi with waffles.

Learning Tip: Your child might miss the **w sound** in the word *always* as it is in
an unstressed second syllable. Help them identify it if necessary.

Is It the W Sound?

Sound out each word. If it **starts** with the **w sound**, color it **pink**.
If it **starts** with another sound, color it yellow.
What word with the **w sound** is in the picture?

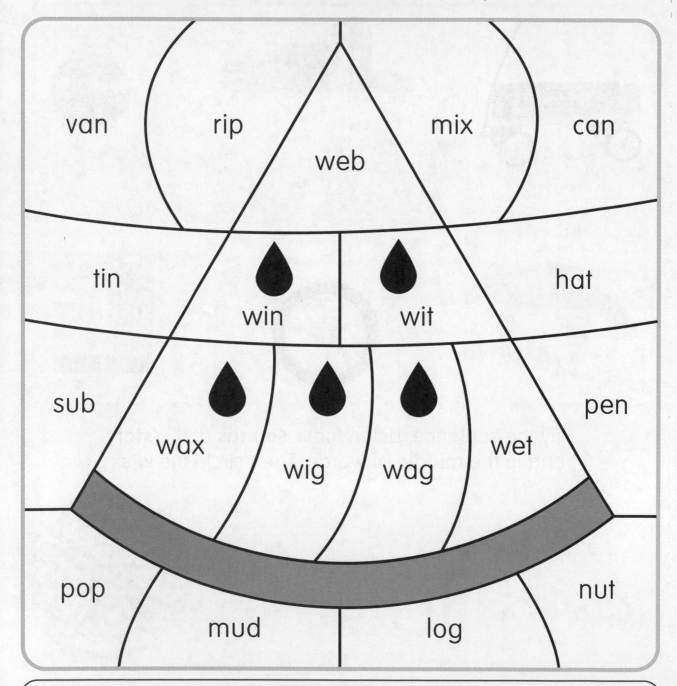

> **Learning Tip:** Assign the **w sound** the action *stand up* and the **r sound** *sit down*.
> Ask your child to do the correct action as you say words that start with these sounds.

W in a Sentence

Say the sentence and listen for 4 **w sounds**.
Then trace the **w**'s, and finish coloring the picture.

The walrus wears a warm sweater.

Learning Tip: Practice linking sounds and letters. Make the **w sound**, and ask your child to make the corresponding letter out of modeling clay or string.

What's Missing?

Say the word for each picture. Then write the letter or letters that stand for the missing sound in each puzzle.

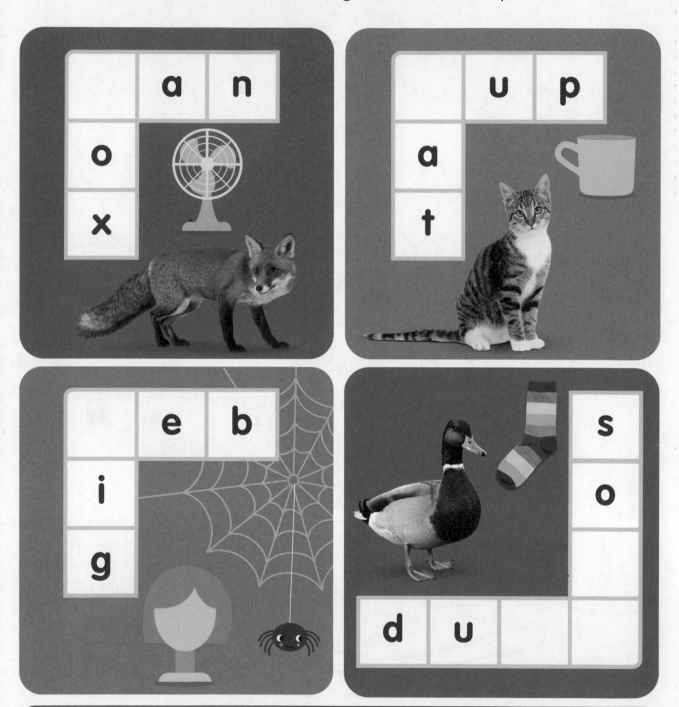

Learning Tip: If your child is struggling to identify the correct sound, encourage them to look back at the words featured on pages 74–89.

90

Follow the Sounds

Sound out the first word and listen for its **first letter sound**.
Then use the key to move to the next box. Follow the path to the finish.

Key: j sound → k sound ↑ f sound ↓ w sound ←

start

jog	jab	fin	jet	fix	ham
dad	pop	fun	cot	fox	bat
fit	wig	wag	cub	fog	lip
jam	jut	jig	cat	fit	hug
pin	pig	box	fob	win	dig
top	bag	mud	job	jot	jar

finish

Learning Tip: Replace the first letter of your child's name and ask them to sound out the new, nonsense name as a fun way to practice different letter sounds.

The Short U Sound

Say each word and listen to the **first sound**.
This is the **short u sound**. Then trace the **u**'s.

up

under

umbrella

Say the words, and circle the 2 that **start** with the **short u sound**.
Cross out the word that doesn't **start** with this sound.

unhappy

us

unicorn

> **Learning Tip:** In the activity above, *us* and *unhappy* start with the **short u sound**, but *unicorn* starts with the **long u sound** (the **u** sounds like the letter's name).

Short U in the Middle

Say each word and listen to the **middle sound**.
This is the **short u sound**. Then trace the **u**'s.

 bus

 sun

 mug

 pup

Say the sentence and listen for 4 **short u sounds**.
Circle them in the sentence.

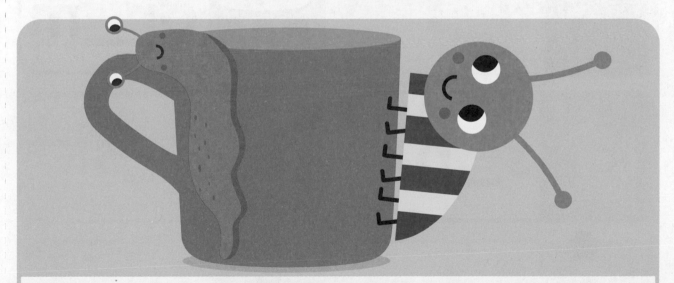

Bug and Slug go up a cup.

Learning Tip: To practice, say pairs of words and ask your child which one has the **short u sound**. E.g., *cat/cut, nut/not, dug/dig, dusk/desk, trick/truck.*

Write Short U

Say each word and listen for the **short u sound**. Then trace the **u**'s.

cub   tub   gum

Write the missing **u** in each word.
Then say the word and listen for the **short u sound**.

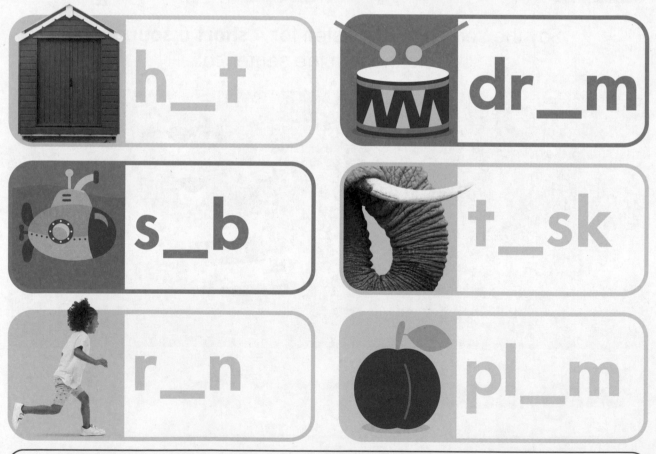

h_t   dr_m

s_b   t_sk

r_n   pl_m

Learning Tip: For extra practice, ask your child to find three **rhyming words** on the page that end with the **-ub sound** and three that end with the **-um sound**.

Short U Puzzle

Sound out each word and listen to the **vowel sound** in the **middle**.
Find and circle 6 words with the **short u sound**.

bun   dot   pat   **hug**

kid   wet

lap   **hum**

gem

hop   bad

rub

beg   **mud**

rip   wig

nut   **fog**

Learning Tip: Use this activity to recap all five **short vowel sounds**. Each word has a short vowel in the middle and is straightforward to sound out.

The V Sound

Say the words and listen for the **v sound**. Then trace the **v**'s.

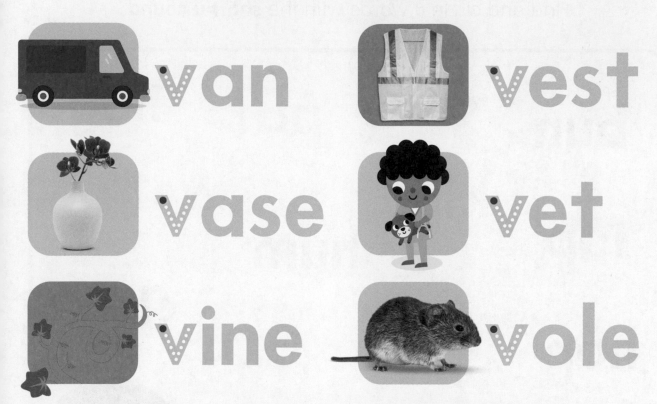

van

vest

vase

vet

vine

vole

Make the **v sound**. Then sound out these words.

vat	vex	vid
vet	veg	van

Learning Tip: Ask your child to put their hand gently on their throat as they make the **v sound**. They should feel their throat vibrate slightly.

Find the V Sound

Say the word for each picture. Where is the **v sound**?
Draw a line to show whether the **v sound** is at the **start** or **end**.

start

end

5

Say the sentence. Listen for **v sounds** at the **start**, **middle**, and **end** of words. Then circle the **v**'s.

Victor and Vivian have seven violins.

Learning Tip: Point out to your child that words ending with the **v sound** are usually spelled with a **silent e** after the **v** (e.g., *have*, *glove*).

V in the Middle

Say the word for each picture.
Circle the word if you hear the **v sound** in the **middle**.

oven

shovel

motorcycle

octopus

noodles

oval

rocket

river

turtle

avocado

Learning Tip: Draw out the **v sound** in each word to sound like a revving engine. If your child has toy cars, they could push them and speed up as they "rev" the **v sound**.

Listen for V

Read the words aloud and listen for the **v sound**.
Then draw lines to match the words to the pictures.

vulture

hive

dive

beaver

violet

wave

Learning Tip: When you are out and about and see items that begin with **v**, say the word and ask your child what sound they hear at the start of the word.

The Y Sound

Say the words and listen for the **y sound**. Then trace the **y**'s.

yak yeti

yarn yolk

yam yard

Make the **y sound**. Then sound out these words.

yes	yap	yip
yet	yum	yell

Learning Tip: This page introduces words where the letter **y** stands for the **y sound**. **Y** can also stand for the **long i sound** (page 148) or the **long e sound** (page 145).

Find the Y Sound

Say the word for each picture. Does it **start** with the **y sound**?
Draw a line from the words that **start** with the **y sound** to the **y**'s.

Say the sentence. Listen for **y sounds** at the **start** and
in the **middle** of words. Then circle the **y**'s.

Yasmin has a yellow yo-yo.

Learning Tip: Point out that in the word *yo-yo*, the letter **y** stands for the **y sound**,
and in this case, it appears in the middle of the word, as well as at the start.

Listen for Y

In each row, say the first word and listen for the **y sound**. Then name the other pictures. Color the one that **starts** with the **y sound**.

yellow

yawn

yoga

Learning Tip: Practice the **y sound** at the supermarket. Ask your child to find and name foods that start with **y** and then say *y-y-yum* or *y-y-yuck* to each one.

Start or Middle?

Say each word and listen for the **y sound**. If it **starts** with a **y sound**, circle it in **blue**. If it has a **y sound** in the **middle**, circle it in **red**.

yes

yarn

yam

lanyard

canyon

yell

Learning Tip: Scramble the letters in a word on this page, and ask your child to unscramble them and say the word. This helps them notice the position of the **y sound**.

The Z Sound

Say the words and listen for the **z sound**. Then trace the **z**'s.

zipper

zebra

zoo

ZOO

Make the **z sound**. Then sound out these words.

zen	zip	zap
zag	zig	zit

Learning Tip: Write **v**, **y**, and **z** on pieces of paper. Say words starting with each sound, and ask your child to tap the paper with the first sound they hear.

Z Sound Puzzle

Trace each line to match the picture with the word.
Then say the word and listen for the **z sound**. Trace the **z**'s.

buzz

zoom

sneeze

fizz

Learning Tip: *Buzz, fizz,* and *zoom* are onomatopoeic (the words sound like their meanings). Onomatopoeic words can help familiarize children with the **z sound**.

S and the Z Sound

Say the words and listen for the **z sound**. Then trace the **s**'s.

rose

hose

girls

dogs

eyes

nose

Say the sentence. Listen for **z sounds** in the **middle** and at the **end** of words. Then circle the 4 **s**'s.

Rosie and Masie are busy bees.

Buzz!

Buzz!

Learning Tip: It is helpful for your child to understand the link between the letter **s** and the **z** sound because **s** stands for the **z sound** more frequently than the letter **z** does.

How Is It Spelled?

Say each word and listen for the **z sound**.
Then circle **s** or **z** to show how the **z sound** is spelled.

zero **S** **Z**

cheese **S** **Z**

daisy **S** **Z**

zigzag **S** **Z**

prize **S** **Z**

birds **S** **Z**

Learning Tip: The **z sound** is voiced and vibrates the tongue slightly (e.g., *dogs*), whereas the **s sound** is a voiceless hiss (e.g., *cats*).

The Zh Sound

Say the words and listen for the **zh sound**.
Then trace the letters that stand for the **zh sound**.

trea**s**ure	
camoufla**ge**	
mea**s**ure	
colla**ge**	
televi**s**ion	

Learning Tip: In English, the **zh sound** is never represented by the letters **zh**.
On this page, we focus on the **s** and **ge spellings** of the **zh sound**.

Is It Zh or Z?

Say each pair of words. Circle the word with a **zh sound** in **red**.
Circle the word with a **z sound** in **purple**.

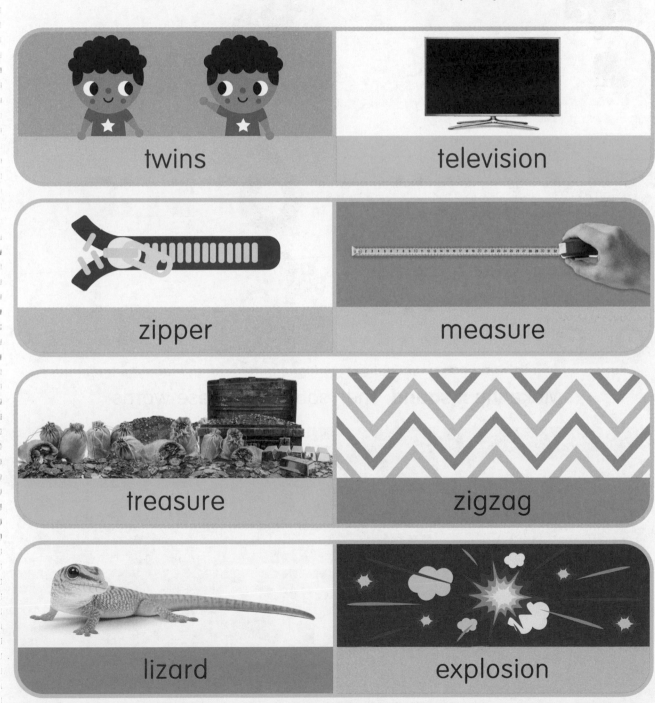

twins

television

zipper

measure

treasure

zigzag

lizard

explosion

Learning Tip: The **zh sound** is one of the hardest sounds to learn. Your child may need to practice this sound more than others before they can say and hear it correctly.

The X Sound

Say the words and listen for the **x sound**. Then trace the **x**'s.

fox

ox

box

six

taxi

sax

Make the **x sound**. Then sound out these words.

tux	fix	max
vex	pox	wax

Learning Tip: This page introduces words in which the letter **x** stands for the **ks sound**. Sometimes, it can also stand for the **gz sound** (e.g., *exit, exam, exist*).

X at the End

Say the word for each picture. If it **ends** with the **x sound**, draw a line from the picture to the **x**'s.

Learning Tip: If your child is struggling to say words with **x** at the end, ask them to practice the **k** and **s sounds** separately, before blending them to say the **x sound**.

The QU Sound

Say the words and listen for the **qu sound**. Then trace the **qu**'s.

question

quail

quack

Say the word for each picture. Does it **start** with the **qu sound**?
Draw lines from the words that **start** with the **qu sound** to the **q**'s.

Learning Tip: Draw your child's attention to the fact that the **qu sound** is a combination of the **k** and **w sounds**. It is spelled using two letters (**q** and **u**).

QU in a Sentence

Say the sentence and listen for 4 **qu sounds**.
Then circle the **qu**'s, and finish coloring the picture.

Queen Quinn took a quick quiz.

Learning Tip: Occasionally, the letter **q** on its own can stand for the **k sound**, e.g., the country names *Qatar* and *Iraq*.

Phonics Wall Chart

Say the word for each picture. Finish coloring the page.
Then pull it out and hang it on your wall.

m sound	short a sound	t sound	s sound
s sound (c at start)	p sound	short i sound	d sound
n sound	h sound	short o sound	b sound
r sound	l sound	g sound	j sound

Learning Tip: Once your child has done the activities on pages 113–116, help them pull out 114 and 115 along the perforations and hang them where they'll see them often.

Phonics Wall Chart

Say the word for each picture. Finish coloring the page.
Then pull it out and hang it on your wall.

j sound (**g** at start)	**short e** sound	**f** sound	**k** sound
k sound (**ck** at end)	**k** sound (**c** at start)	**w** sound	**short u** sound
v sound	**y** sound	**z** sound	**z** sound (**s** near end)
zh sound (middle **s**)	**x** sound (at end)	**z** sound (**x** at start)	**qu** sound

Learning Tip: Use the examples in this chart to test your child's understanding of letter sounds. E.g., ask your child, "What sound does giraffe start with?"

The SH Sound

Say the words and listen for the **sh sound**. Then trace the **sh**'s.

shark

ship

sheep

Make the **sh sound**. Then sound out these words.

shed	shut	shot
shop	shin	shift

Learning Tip: To teach this sound, put a finger over your mouth and say *shhhh*, as if you're asking someone to be quiet. Ask your child to do this, too. Then say *shhh-ark*.

SH at the End

Say each word and listen for the **sh sound**.
Then draw lines to match the words to the pictures.

hush

blush

mash

dish

splash

push

Learning Tip: Even though the **sh sound** is often written using two letters, it is a single sound. When two letters stand for one sound, the letter pair is called a **digraph**.

Find the SH Sound

Circle the words that **start** with the **sh sound** in **purple**.
Circle the words that **end** with the **sh sound** in **red**.

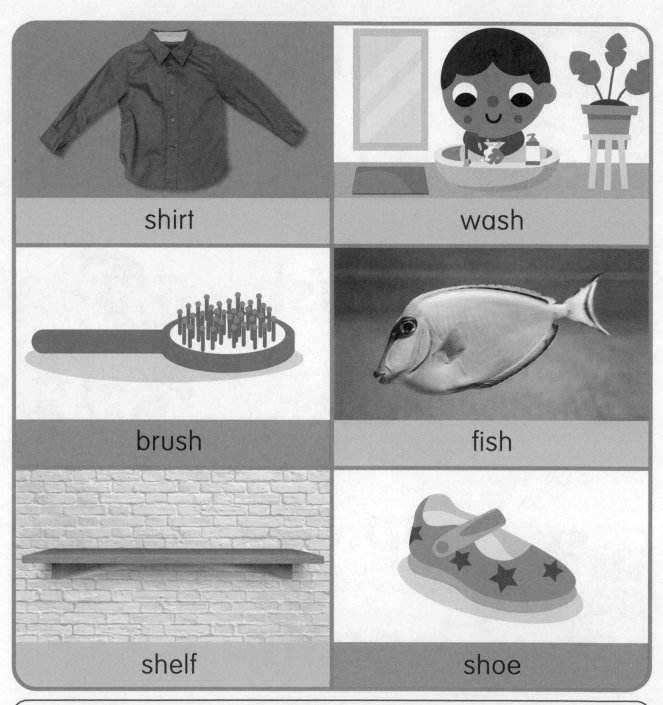

shirt

wash

brush

fish

shelf

shoe

Learning Tip: In English, the **sh sound** is usually made with the letters **sh**. However, the **sh sound** can be written in other ways, e.g., *oce*an, *ch*ef, *st*ation, *musi*cian.

Is It SH or S?

Say the tongue twister a few times.
Circle the letters that stand for the **sh sound** in **red**.
Circle the letters that stand for the **s sound** in **green**.

She sells seashells on the seashore.

Learning Tip: This tongue twister can be difficult for young children, so make a fun game of it. (Note: the **s** at the end of *sells* and *seashells* has the **z sound**, see pages 106–107.)

The CH Sound

Say the words and listen for the **ch sound**. Then trace the **ch**'s.

chase

cheese

chick

Make the **ch sound**. Then sound out these words.

chat	chill	chin
chop	chap	chug

Learning Tip: To teach this sound, say *choo, choo*, as if you're pretending to be a train. Ask your child to do it, too. Then say *ch-ch-chair*.

CH at the End

Say each word and listen for the **ch sound**.
Then draw lines to match the words to the pictures.

lunch

couch

bench

branch

peach

beach

Learning Tip: In English, the **ch sound** is usually made with the letters **ch**. However, the sound can also be made with the letters **tu**. E.g., *nature, century*.

121

Find the CH Sound

Circle the words that **start** with the **ch sound** in **red**.
Circle the words that **end** with the **ch sound** in **purple**.

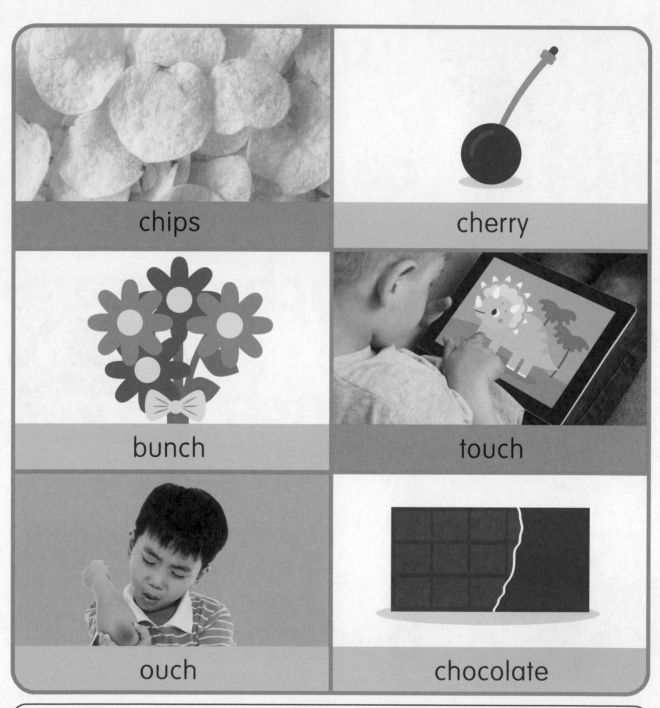

chips

cherry

bunch

touch

ouch

chocolate

Learning Tip: For an extra activity, write the word *church* and ask your child to identify where the **ch sound** is. Can they find it at the start and end of the word?

Write CH

Write the missing **ch** in each word.
Then say the word and listen for the **ch sound**.

 __ __ ess

 __ __ ili

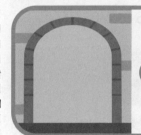 ri __ __

 tea __ __

 ar __ __

 pun __ __

 __ __ ain

 __ __ alk

Learning Tip: For extra practice, ask your child to name five words that start with **ch**. Give hints if necessary.

Unvoiced TH Sound

Say the words and listen for the **unvoiced th sound**.
Then trace the **th**'s.

thump

think

Thump!

thank

Make the **unvoiced th sound**. Then sound out these words.

thin	thick
thing	thorn

Learning Tip: The **unvoiced th sound** is also called the **voiceless** or **soft th sound**. It usually comes at the start of nouns, verbs, and adjectives (e.g., *theater, think, thirsty*).

End Unvoiced TH

Say each word and listen for the **unvoiced th sound**.
Then draw lines to match the words to the pictures.

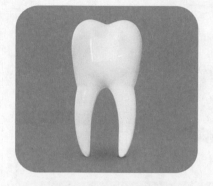

bath

path

moth

math

mouth

tooth

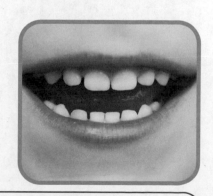

Learning Tip: The letters **th** are often **unvoiced** when they come at the end of a word or before a consonant (e.g., *cloth, bathtub*).

Find Unvoiced TH

Circle the words that **start** with the **unvoiced th sound** in **red**.
Circle the words that **end** with the **unvoiced th sound** in **pink**.

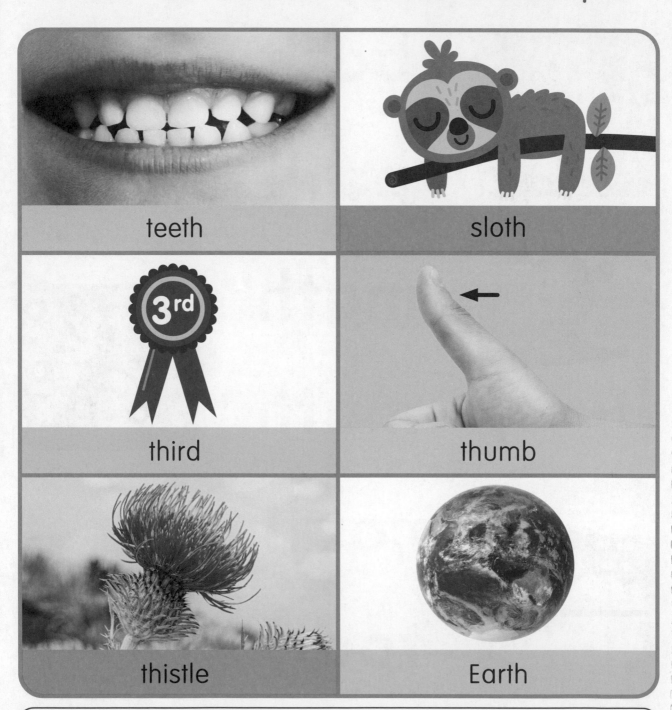

teeth

sloth

third

thumb

thistle

Earth

Learning Tip: Children sometimes replace the **unvoiced th sound** with the **f sound**.
Help your child hear the difference between the first sounds in *three* and *four*.

Unvoiced TH Puzzle

Say each word. If it has an **unvoiced th sound** at the **start**, color that part **blue**. If it has an **unvoiced th sound** at the **end**, color that part **orange**. What word with the **unvoiced th sound** is in the picture?

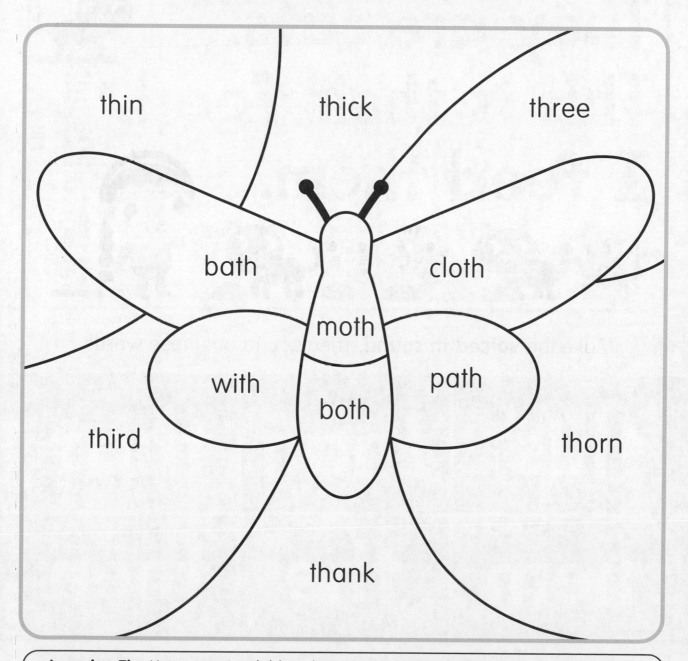

thin   thick   three

bath   cloth

moth

with   path

both

third   thorn

thank

Learning Tip: Listen to your child as they say each word in the puzzle to make sure they are saying it correctly. Praise their effort and gently correct any mistakes.

Voiced TH Sound

Say the words and listen for the **voiced th sound**.
Then trace the **th**'s.

They are cats.
This is their food.
I feed them.

Make the **voiced th sound**. Then sound out these words.

this	than	that
them	the	then

Learning Tip: The **voiced th sound** is also known as the **hard th sound**. It usually comes at the start of function words (words without meanings we can picture). E.g., *this, they, than.*

Middle Voiced TH

Say each word and listen for the **voiced th sound**.
Then draw lines to match the words to the pictures.

brother

feather

clothes

father

mother

breathe

Learning Tip: The **voiced th sound** rarely appears at the end of words without being followed by a **silent e**, but one exception is *smooth*.

Find Voiced TH

Say the words. Where is the **voiced th sound**? Circle the words with the **voiced th sound** at the **start** in **green**. Circle the words with the **voiced th sound** in the **middle** in **purple**.

that

mother

them

clothing

the

father

slither

this

Learning Tip: Sometimes **th** can stand for the **t sound**, e.g., *Thomas*. When **th** is split over two syllables, both the **t sound** and the **h sound** are heard, e.g., *foothill*.

Voiced TH Puzzle

Say each word and listen for the **voiced th sound**.
Then find and circle it in the word search.

them   they   gather   other   than   this

s	m	a	p	t	m	o	a	q	h
q	t	d	t	w	s	t	p	n	d
u	h	v	l	k	m	h	r	t	t
i	a	n	g	w	i	e	i	h	b
o	n	a	i	g	q	r	d	y	n
g	a	t	h	e	r	l	p	n	q
s	f	m	l	u	r	s	i	q	z
t	h	e	m	i	i	t	h	i	s
i	g	a	t	d	n	r	a	d	e
r	w	t	h	e	y	q	x	b	c

Learning Tip: Ask your child to put a hand lightly over their throat to feel how it **vibrates** slightly with **voiced th sounds** but not unvoiced ones.

The NG Sound

Say the words and listen for the **ng sound**. Then trace the **ng**'s.

sing king

wing ring

gong bang

Make the **ng sound**. Then sound out these words.

lung	rang	clang
sang	long	song

Learning Tip: In English, the **ng sound** never occurs at the start of a word. It always follows a vowel sound.

Find the NG Sound

Say the sentences and listen for the **ng sounds**.
Then circle the 5 **ng sounds**, and finish coloring the picture.

Bang!

The king banged the gong. It rang for a long time.

Learning Tip: Many **ng sound** words are onomatopoeic (they sound like their meaning). Let your child have fun with words such as *bong*, *gong*, *clang*, and *bang*.

133

The NK Sound

Say the words and listen for the **nk sound**. Then trace the **nk**'s.

ink

sink

wink

bunk

pink

Oink!

oink

Make the **nk sound**. Then sound out these words.

sunk	bank	tank
honk	link	stink

Learning Tip: The **nk sound** is a blend of two other sounds: the **ng sound** and the **k sound**. Help your child say both sounds and then run them together.

Write NK

Write the missing **nk** in each word.
Then say the word and listen for the **nk sound**.

 thi__ __

 pla__ __

 sa__ __

 bli__ __

 du__ __

 ri__ __

 tru__ __

 dri__ __

Learning Tip: Let your child know that when the letters **nk** appear in a word, the **n** always has the **ng sound**.

135

Two-Letter Sounds

Say the word for each picture, and draw a line
to show whether it has the **sh**, **ch**, **ng**, or **nk sound**.

Learning Tip: Make sure your child is aware that the featured sounds aren't all at the
start of the word. Some are at the end.

Trace and Match

Say each word. Then trace the two-letter sound, and draw a line to match the word to its picture.

sheep

cheese

tooth

clothes

wing

tank

Learning Tip: For extra practice, ask your child what other sounds they can hear when they name the objects on this page.

The Long A Sound

Say each word and listen to the **first sound**. This is the **long a sound**. Then trace the letters that stand for the **long a sound**.

ape   ache

ace   alien

Say the words, and circle the 2 that **start** with the **long a sound**. Cross out the 2 that don't **start** with this sound.

apple

apron

acorn

astronaut

Learning Tip: In the activity above, *apron* and *acorn* start with the **long a sound**, but *apple* and *astronaut* start with the **short a sound** (see page 8).

The AY Spelling

When the **long a sound** is at the **end** of a word, we often spell it **ay**. Say each word and listen to the **last sound**. Then trace **ay**.

hay   tray

pay   gray

Say the sentence and listen for 4 **long a sounds**.
Circle them in the sentence.

Today, Jay plays with clay.

Learning Tip: Long vowel sounds sound like the name of the letter. They can be spelled several ways. This section introduces the most common ways.

139

The AI Spelling

Sound out the words. When you see **ai**, make the **long a sound**. Then trace the **ai**'s, and match the words to the pictures.

rain

mail

sail

train

snail

paint

Learning Tip: The **ai** spelling often stands for the **long a sound**. While it usually sits in the middle of a word, it can also be at the start, e.g., *aim* and *aid*.

The A_E Spelling

Say the words and listen for the **long a sound**.
Then trace the letters that stand for the **long a sound**.

cake   tape

gate   lake

Say each pair of words. Circle the word with a **long a sound** in **blue**.
Circle the word with a **short a sound** in **red**.

man   ←mane

can   cane

Learning Tip: A final **silent e** tells us that the **vowel** before it has a **long vowel sound**.
To hear this, say pairs of words such as *tap/tape, mad/made, plan/plane*.

The Long E Sound

Say each word and listen to the **first sound**. This is the **long e sound**.
Trace the letters that stand for the **long e sound**.

eat   east

eel   equal

Say the words, and circle the 2 that **start** with the **long e sound**.
Cross out the 2 that don't **start** with this sound.

eagle   email   engine   egg

Learning Tip: In the activity above, *eagle* and *email* start with the **long e sound**, but *egg* and *engine* start with the **short e sound** (see page 70).

The EE Spelling

Sound out the words. When you see **ee**, make the **long e sound**. Then trace the **ee**'s, and match the words to the pictures.

bee

feet

tree

sheep

queen

three

3

Learning Tip: The **long e sound** is pronounced like the name of the letter **e**. It is a longer sound than the **short e sound**. E.g., compare *meet* (long e) with *met* (short e).

The EA Spelling

Sound out each word. When you see the letters **ea**, make the **long e sound**. Then trace the **ea**'s.

Say each pair of words. Circle the word with a **long e sound** in **orange**. Circle the word with a **short e sound** in **purple**.

beds

beads

steam

stem

Learning Tip: Many words that sound the same but have different meanings (homophones) have the **ee** and **ea spellings**. E.g., *see/sea, week/weak, meet/meat.*

The Final Y

Sound out the words. When you see the letter **y**, make the **long e sound**. Then draw lines to match the words to the pictures.

rainy

kitty

mommy

daddy

bunny

sunny

Learning Tip: Here, the letter **y** is a vowel that stands for the **long e sound**. It can also stand for other vowel sounds, such as the **short i sound**. E.g., *gym, system, myth*.

The Long I Sound

Say each word and listen to the **first sound**.
This is the **long i sound**. Then trace the **i**'s.

ivy   iron

idea

I

Say the words, and circle the 2 that **start** with the **long i sound**.
Cross out the 2 that don't **start** with this sound.

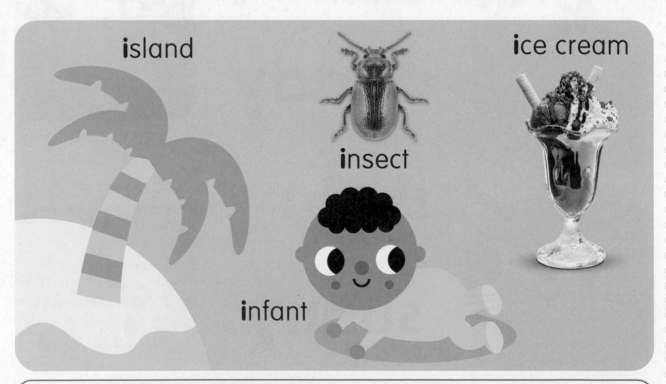

island   ice cream

insect

infant

Learning Tip: In the activity above, *island* and *ice cream* start with the **long i sound**, but *infant* and *insect* start with the **short i sound** (see page 26).

The I_E Spelling

Say the words and listen for the **long i sound**. Then trace the letters that stand for the **long i sound**.

kite   bike

mice   rice

Say each pair of words. Circle the word with a long i sound in blue. Circle the word with a **short i sound** in **red**.

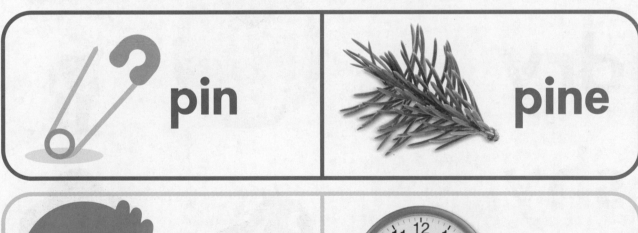

pin   pine

Tim   time

Learning Tip: A final **silent e** tells us that the **vowel** before it has a **long vowel sound**. To hear this, say pairs of words such as *slid/slide, kit/kite, rid/ride*.

The Final Y

Sound out the words. When you see **y**, make the **long i sound**. Then trace the **y**'s, and match the words to the pictures.

cry

fly

spy

dry

shy

why

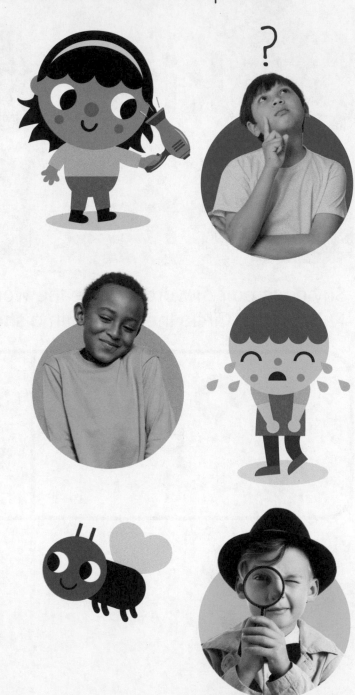

> **Learning Tip:** When **y** is the **first or only vowel**, it often stands for the **long i sound** (e.g., *type*). If the **y** is **unstressed**, it stands for the **long e sound** (e.g., *turkey*).

Just I

Sound out the words. When you see the letter **i**, make the **long i sound**. Then draw lines to match the words to the pictures.

child

blind

bicycle

climb

spider

silent

Learning Tip: When the letter **i** comes **in front of two consonants** or is the **last letter in a syllable** it often stands for the **long i sound**.

The Long O Sound

Say each word and listen to the **first sound**. This is the **long o sound**. Then trace the **o**'s.

over   open

oval   okay

Say the words, and circle the 2 that **start** with the **long o sound**. Cross out the 2 that don't **start** with this sound.

octopus

overalls

ostrich

ocean

Learning Tip: In the activity above, *overalls* and *ocean* start with the **long o sound**, but *ostrich* and *octopus* start with the **short o sound** (see page 44).

The O Spelling

Sound out the words. When you see the letter **o**, make the **long o sound**. Then trace the **o**'s, and match the words to the pictures.

go

no

pony

donut

yogurt

buffalo

GO

Learning Tip: The **long o sound** is pronounced like the name of the letter **o**. It is a longer sound than the **short o sound**. E.g., compare *go* (long o) with *got* (short o).

The O_E Spelling

Say the words and listen for the **long o sound**.
Then trace the letters that stand for the **long o sound**.

rope   home

nose   doze

Say the sentence and listen for 3 **long o sounds**.
Circle them in the sentence.

Rose chose new clothes.

Learning Tip: Remind your child that when a vowel is followed by a consonant and then a **silent e**, the first vowel is usually pronounced as a **long vowel sound**.

OA and OW Spellings

Sound out the words. When you see the letters **oa** or **ow**, make the **long o sound**. Then draw lines to match the words to the pictures.

soap

snow

boat

mow

pillow

toad

> **Learning Tip:** The **oa spelling** of the **long o sound** usually falls in the **middle** of a word, while the **ow spelling** often falls at the **end** of a word.

The Long U Sound

Say each word and listen to the **first sound**. This is the **long u sound**. Then trace the **u**'s.

unicorn

uniform

Say the words, and circle the 2 that **start** with the **long u sound**. Cross out the 2 that don't **start** with this sound.

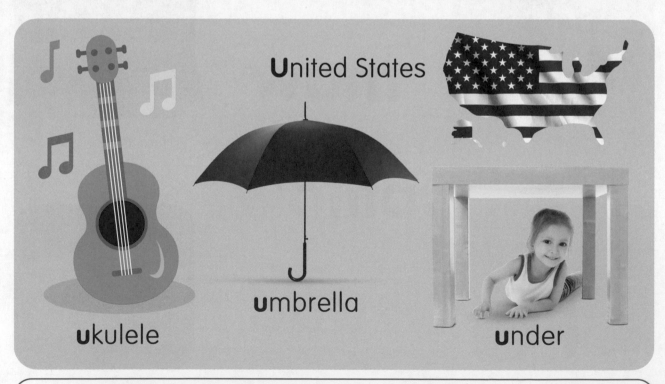

United States

ukulele

umbrella

under

Learning Tip: In the activity above, *ukulele* and *United States* start with the **long u sound**, but *umbrella* and *under* start with the **short u sound** (see page 92).

The U_E Spelling

Say the words and listen for the **long u sound**.
Then trace the letters that stand for the **long u sound**.

cube   cute

mule   puke

Say the sentence and listen for 3 **long u sounds**.
Circle them in the sentence.

Hugo plays a huge bugle.

Learning Tip: In many places, words such as *tube* and *new* are pronounced with the
long oo sound, not the long u sound (see pages 157 and 234).

Just U

Say each word. When you see the letter **u** make the **long u sound**.
Then draw a line to match the word to the picture.

emu

bugle

human

pupil

fuel

menu

Learning Tip: While it may seem hard to know which words have the **long u** and which have the **short u**, fewer have the **long u sound** and the key ones soon become familiar.

Long U or Long OO?

Sometimes the letters **u, ew,** and **u_e** stand for the **long u sound** and sometimes they stand for the **long oo sound**, as in *boot*. Say each word, and draw a line to either **long u** or **long oo**.

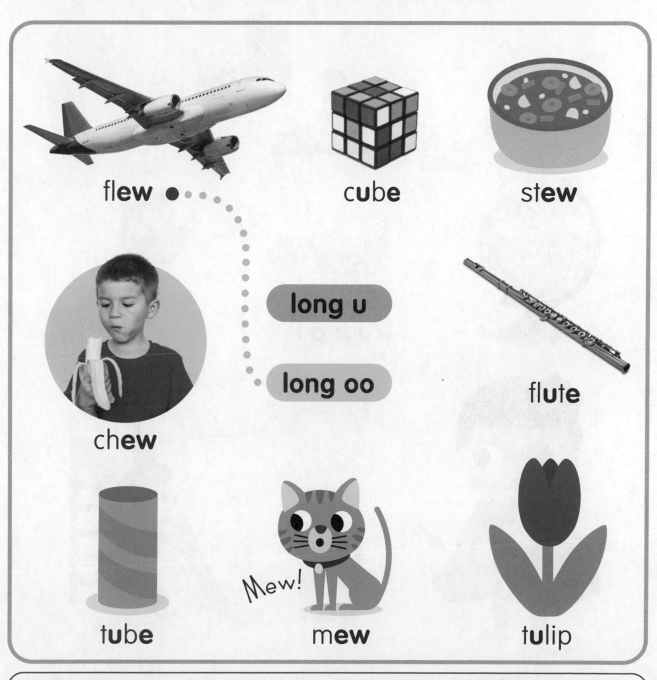

fl**ew**

c**u**b**e**

st**ew**

long u

long oo

fl**u**t**e**

ch**ew**

t**u**b**e**

Mew!

m**ew**

t**u**lip

Learning Tip: Whether a word is pronounced with the **long u** or **long oo sound** can vary. Help your child draw lines that represent how you say the words.

Which Long Vowel?

Say the word for each picture and listen for the **long vowel sound**.
Draw a line from the picture to the sound.

long a

long i

long o

5

Learning Tip: There are no labels on these pictures so children will need to listen to each word to figure out its **long vowel sound**, rather than use the letters as clues.

158

Find the Rhymes

Say the words and listen for the **middle** and **end sounds**. Then draw lines to match the words that **rhyme**.

nose

fire

hike

grape

snake

hose

cake

bike

tape

wire

Learning Tip: This page and the next one practice the **silent e** learning point: we use the **long vowel sound** when a vowel is followed by consonant and then a **silent e**.

Unscramble the Words

Say the word for each picture. Then unscramble the letters to write the word. All the words have a **long vowel sound** and a final **silent e**.

eimc

__ __ __ __

ober

__ __ __ __

kela

__ __ __ __

oten

__ __ __ __

ceub

__ __ __ __

kera

__ __ __ __

Learning Tip: If your child finds this hard, ask them to write an **e** at the end of each word. Then mention that the **long vowel** will be the second letter.

Join the Words

Draw a line joining the 3 words with the **long a sound**.
Draw a line joining the 3 words with the **long i sound**.
Draw a line joining the 3 words with the **long o sound**.
Draw a line joining the 3 words with the **long u sound**.

brave   make

mine   broke

fume   use   ride

froze   cute

hope   shine

game

Learning Tip: Encourage your child to say each word and listen for the **long vowel sound**. If necessary, remind them that the **final e** is **silent**.

Long Vowel Practice

Sound out the words and listen for the **long vowel sound**.
Then draw lines to match the words to the pictures.

tail

rope

huge

leash

cry

Learning Tip: This activity includes one word for each **long vowel sound**.
Help your child identify which **long vowel sound** each word has.

Long Vowel Practice

Say the words and listen for the **vowel sounds**.
Write an **L** beside the words with a **long vowel sound**.
Write an **S** by the words with a **short vowel sound**.

feed [L]

hive ☐

duck ☐

jay ☐

skates ☐

fox ☐

music ☐

try ☐

bag ☐

throw ☐

Learning Tip: Help your child listen to the sound of each word to figure out if it has a **long vowel sound**. After that, discuss any spelling patterns they have already learned.

TCH as the CH Sound

Say the words and listen for the **ch sound**. Then trace the **tch**'s.

watch

patch

hatch

Make the **ch sound**. Then sound out these words.

batch

fetch

hutch

pitch

Learning Tip: In English, three letters can sometimes stand for one sound. This page teaches words in which **tch** stands for the **ch sound**.

Write TCH

Write the missing **tch** in each word.
Then say the word and listen for the **tch** sound.

w a _ _ _

i _ _ _

m a _ _ _

c a _ _ _

p i _ _ _ e r

k e _ _ _ u p

Learning Tip: If the **ch sound** comes immediately after a **short vowel sound**, it is usually spelled with the letters **tch** rather than **ch**.

165

WR as the R Sound

Say the words and listen for the **r sound**. Then trace the **wr**'s.

wrapper

wren

wreck

Make the **r sound**. Then sound out these words.

wrench	wring
wrong	wrote

Learning Tip: Help your child understand that the letters **wr** make the **r sound** and that **wr** is a **digraph**, where two letters stand for one sound.

R Sound Puzzle

Trace each line to match the picture with the word.
Then say the word, listen for the **r sound**, and trace the **wr**'s.

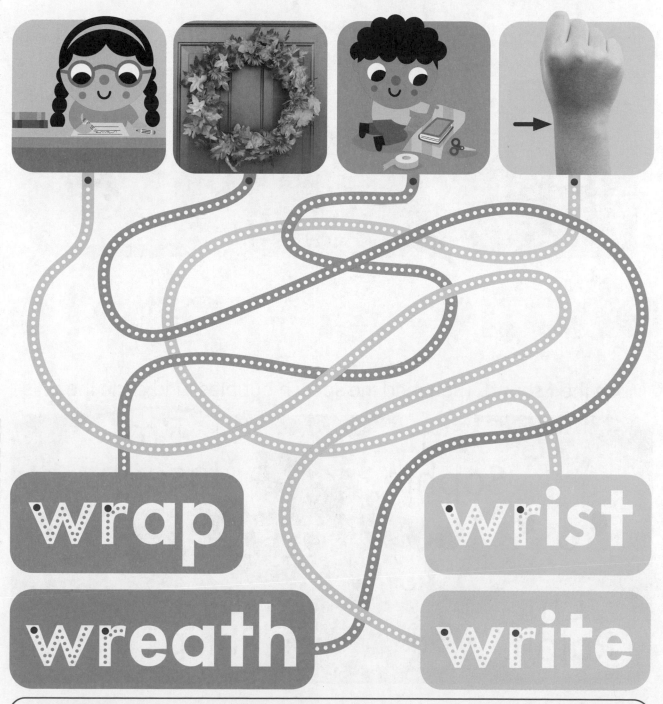

wrap

wreath

wrist

write

Learning Tip: Many **wr** words relate in some way to twisting, turning, or reshaping. E.g., *wrapping* involves reshaping; the *wrist* twists the hand; and *writing* is a twisting line.

PH as the F Sound

Say the words and listen for the **f sound**. Then trace the **ph**'s.

dolphin

phone

photo

Make the **f sound**. Then read the speech bubbles, and circle the **ph**'s.

> **Learning Tip:** Point out to your child that the **ph digraph** can appear at the **start** (*ph*one), in the **middle** (*dol*ph*in*), or at the **end** of a word (*Joseph*).

PH in the Middle

Say the word for each picture and listen for the **f sound**. If you hear it, find and circle the **ph** letters that stand for the **f sound**.

xylophone

dinosaur

microphone

alphabet

truck

pumpkin

elephant

headphones

Learning Tip: Words with **ph** in the middle often have the same root word. E.g., *headphones*, *xylophone*, and *microphone* all share the root word *phone*.

GH as the F Sound

Say the words and listen for the **f sound**. Then trace the **gh**'s.

Ha-ha!

laugh

rough

Say the words, and circle the word with the **f sound** at the end.
Cross out the 2 words that don't contain the **f sound**.

light

cough

eight

Learning Tip: The letters **gh** can be difficult to read because they can stand for the **f sound**, but they can also be silent, as in the words *light* and *eight*.

Is It GH or PH?

Say the word for each picture and listen for the **f sound**.
Then circle **gh** or **ph** to show how the **f sound** is spelled.

Ha-ha!

laugh **gh ph**

trough **gh ph**

elephant **gh ph**

photo **gh ph**

tough **gh ph**

phone **gh ph**

Learning Tip: If your child is ready, discuss how the word *photo* is short for *photograph* and how *photograph* has the **ph** spelling at the start and end.

DGE as the J Sound

Say the words and listen for the **j sound**. Then trace the **dge**'s.

bridge

fudge

badge

Make the **j sound**. Then sound out these words.

ledge	dodge
ridge	budge

Learning Tip: In English, a **j sound** at the **end** of a word is usually represented by the letters **dge** (*badge*) or **ge** (*garage*).

172

Listen for J

Read the words aloud and listen for the **j sound**. Then trace the **dge**'s, and draw lines to match the words to the pictures.

fridge

hedge

badger

judge

wedge

Learning Tip: If the **j sound** follows a short vowel and falls at the end of a word or at the start of a syllable, it usually has the **dge** spelling.

KN as the N Sound

Say the words and listen for the **n sound**. Then trace the **kn**'s.

knife

knee

knot

Make the **n sound**. Then sound out these words.

knit	knock
kneel	knack

Learning Tip: Introduce homophones (e.g., *knot/not, know/no*) to reinforce the idea that words can sound the same but have different spellings.

Find the N Sound

Say the words and listen for the **n sound**. Color the letters that stand for the **n sound green**. Color the **other letters orange**.

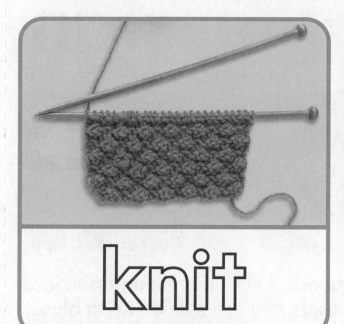

knit

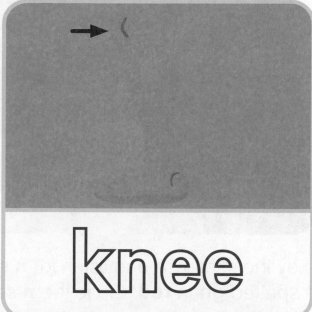

knee

knight

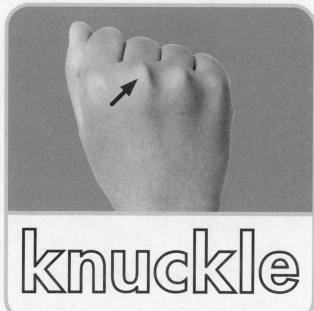

knuckle

Learning Tip: In this activity, coloring both letters that stand for the **n sound** one color reinforces the idea that they stand for one sound.

GN as the N Sound

Say the words and listen for the **n sound**. Then trace the **gn**'s.

gnu   gnome   sign

Say the sentence and listen for **n sounds**. Circle the **n sounds** that are spelled **gn** in **red**. Circle the **n sounds** that are spelled **kn** in **blue**.

The gnu knew not to gnaw on Knox's knitting.

Learning Tip: Check that your child understands the meaning of the words on this page, as well as being able to say them correctly.

Is It GN or KN?

Say each word and listen for the **n sound**. Circle the words with the **gn spelling** in **purple**. Circle the words with the **kn spelling** in **orange**.

gnaw

gnu

knit

knead

kneel

gnomes

gnat

knight

Learning Tip: Teachers may refer to **gn** or **kn** as **graphemes**. Graphemes are written symbols that represent one sound. A two-letter **grapheme** is also called a **digraph**.

WH as the W Sound

Say the words and listen for the **w sound**. Then trace the **wh**'s.

wheat

whale

wheel

Make the **w sound**. Then sound out these words.

whisk

white

whiz

whack

Learning Tip: The letters **wh** used to stand for a **hw sound**. In some places, you can still hear a brief **h sound** before the w when people say words such as *whale* and *wheel*.

Question Match-Up

Say the question words and listen for the **w sound**.
Then trace the lines to match the question word to the ending.

What

Why

When

Where

Which

... is grass green?

... pet is best, cats or dogs?

... do you live?

... is your name?

... will we eat?

Learning Tip: If your child can say and understand common question words, it will help them in all areas of their classroom learning.

Listen and Match

Say the word for each picture. Then draw lines to match the picture to the correct two- or three-letter sound.

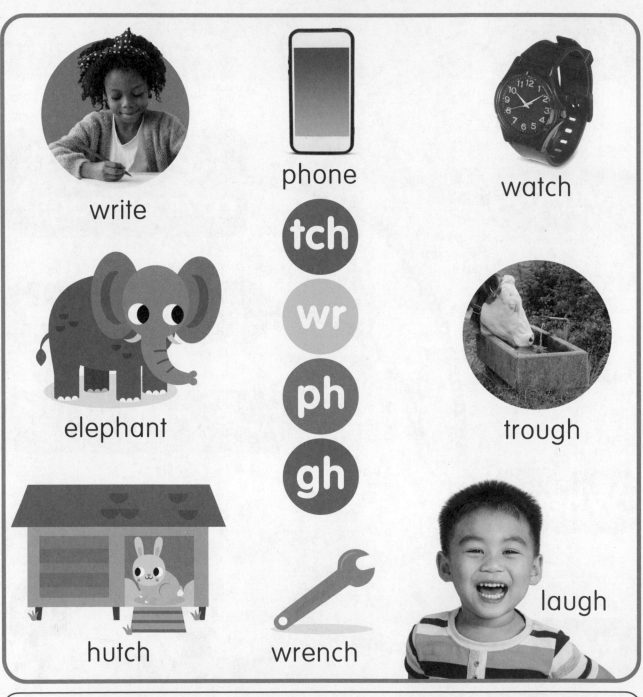

write

phone

watch

tch

wr

ph

gh

elephant

trough

hutch

wrench

laugh

Learning Tip: Repetition reinforces learning. The pictures on pages 180–181 show words that your child has learned earlier in this section.

Trace and Match

Trace the letters in the middle of the page.
Then say the word for each picture, and draw lines to match
the picture to the correct two- or three-letter sound.

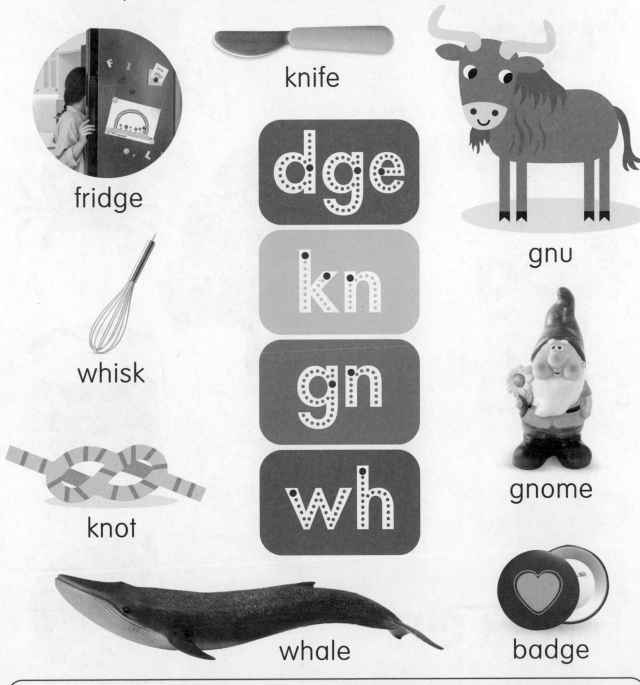

knife

fridge

gnu

dge

kn

gn

wh

whisk

gnome

knot

whale

badge

Learning Tip: Remind your child that **gn** and **kn** both stand for the **n sound**.
In this activity, tracing the letters helps draw attention to the different spellings.

R Blends

Say each word and listen for the **r blend**. Then trace the letters, and match the word to its picture.

tree

grapes

frog

crab

drum

broken

Learning Tip: The words on this page have **initial blends**. The sounds of the first two consonants blend together but both can be heard.

More R Blends

Say each word and listen for the **r blend**. Then circle the letters that make up the blend.

prom

grandma

troll

bride

Say the words. Then circle the word in each pair that **starts** with an **r blend**.

brush

rush

rice

price

Learning Tip: If your child's first language is not English, they may need extra practice identifying the **r sound** and the sounds that make up **r blends**.

Match R Blends

Say the words and listen for the **r blends**. Then draw lines to match the words with the same **r blend**.

bricks

cricket

frozen

grass

drop

bridge

grin

crow

draw

fruit

Learning Tip: In phonics, the term **consonant blend** refers to the spoken form of the consonants, while the term **consonant cluster** refers to the written form.

Hear R Blends

Say the word for each picture and listen for the **r blend**.
Then choose the correct two letters and write them in place.

cr fr gr tr

__ __ a i n

__ __ e e n

__ __ i e s

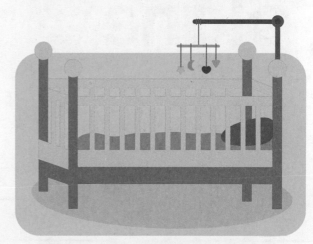

__ __ i b

Learning Tip: If your child is not yet able to write the letters unassisted, discuss which letters are needed, then write them in lightly and allow your child to trace them.

L Blends

Say each word and listen for the **l blend**. Then trace the letters, and match the word to its picture.

black

flap

climb

plane

gloves

slippers

Learning Tip: Each word on this page starts with a different sound, but all the initial sounds blend with **l** to create an **l blend**. Ask your child to identify the six **l blends**.

More L Blends

Say each word and listen for the **l blend**.
Then circle the letters that make up the blend.

cloud

flip flops   planet   slide

Say the words. Then circle the word in each pair
that **starts** with an **l blend**.

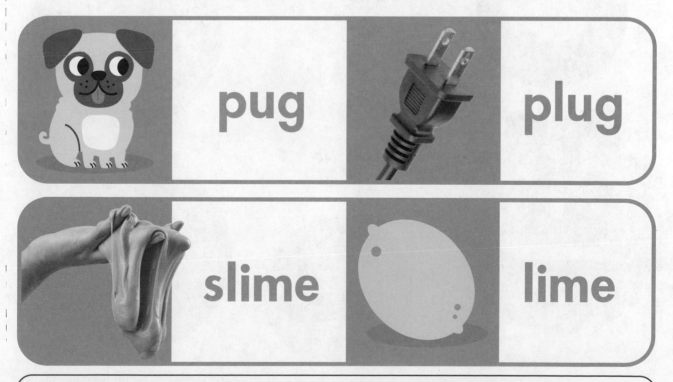

pug   plug

slime   lime

Learning Tip: To help your child hear the blends, discuss word pairs with and without blends, such as *back/black, fame/flame, love/glove, flip/lip, place/lace,* etc.

Match L Blends

Say the words and listen for the **l blends**. Then draw lines to match the words with the same **l blend**.

slice

blue

slip

plum

glue

clam

glass

plant

blocks

clock

Learning Tip: For extra practice, ask your child to name other words that begin with these **l blends**. Alternatively, list two words, and ask which one has the **l blend**.

Hear L Blends

Say the word for each picture and listen for the **l blend**.
Then choose the correct two letters and write them in place.

bl gl cl sl

_ _ e e p   _ _ a s t

_ _ o b e   _ _ a p

Learning Tip: If your child finds this difficult, have fun putting an incorrect blend in front of the letters and asking if it's correct. E.g., for *sleep*, say, "Is it *bleep*?"

189

S Blends

Say each word and listen for the **s blend**. Then trace the letters, and match the word to its picture.

spill

skirt

sneeze

star

swim

smile

Learning Tip: With the **r** and **l blends** on the previous pages, the **r** or **l sound** came second in each word. With **s blends**, the **s sound** is at the start of the words.

More S Blends

Say each word and listen for the **s blend**. Then circle the letters that make up the blend.

spoon

stool

swan

skip

Say the words. Then circle the word in each pair that **starts** with an **s blend**.

sink

stink

nap

Snap!

snap

Learning Tip: Extend these activities by saying the following tongue twister together and then discussing the **s blends** within it: *Six slick, slimy snakes slid slowly south.*

Match S Blends

Say the words and listen for the **s blends**. Then draw lines to match the words with the same **s blend**.

stop

scarf

swing

snack

spines

snore

storm

spots

skunk

sweep

Learning Tip: Although *scarf* is spelled with the consonant cluster **sc**, it has the same **s blend** as *skunk*, because **sc** and **sk** sound the same.

Hear S Blends

Say the word for each picture and listen for the **s blend**.
Then choose the correct two letters and write them in place.

sk sn sp sm

_ _ a k e

_ _ a t e

_ _ i n

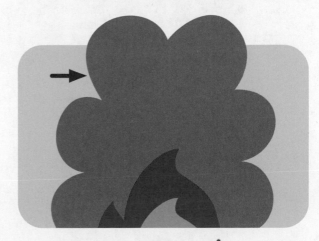

_ _ o k e

Learning Tip: Help your child use both the letters and the picture to figure out the correct word. Then ask them to listen to the word to figure out the **s blend**.

The TW Blend

Say the words and listen for the **tw blend**.
Then trace the **tw**'s.

twins

twenty

Tweet!

tweet

twirl

twig

tweed

Learning Tip: Have fun practicing the **tw blend** with your child by pretending to be owls and making the sound *twit, twit, twoo; twit, twit, twoo.*

More TW Blends

Trace each line to match the word with the picture.
Say the word and listen for the **tw blend**. Then trace the **tw**.

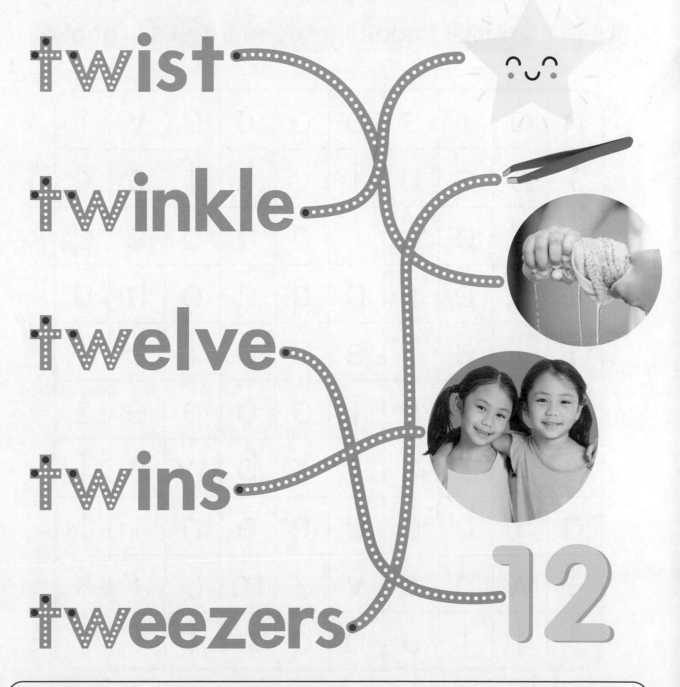

twist

twinkle

twelve

twins

tweezers

Learning Tip: Many words with the **tw blend** relate to two in some way (e.g., *twice*, *be**tw**een*). In the word *two*, the **w** is silent, but the word has the same origins.

The QU Blend

Sound out each word and listen for the **qu blend**.
Then find and circle it in the word search.

quilt   quick   quail   queen   quiz   quake

h	a	i	s	b	g	c	a	v	t
f	o	q	u	i	c	k	j	z	c
r	d	u	w	r	a	o	d	e	q
e	x	e	k	p	q	n	o	h	u
l	t	a	r	e	u	a	l	t	i
q	u	s	n	j	a	o	p	e	z
u	m	r	a	t	k	b	w	s	l
a	t	b	q	u	e	e	n	l	t
i	w	n	e	v	z	m	q	i	s
l	t	l	a	b	q	u	i	l	t

Learning Tip: This page builds on pages 112–113. Remind your child that the letters **qu** stand for a blend of the **k** and **w** sounds. (Exceptions include *unique* and *boutique*.)

The SQU Blend

Say the words, and trace the **squ**'s.
Then draw lines to match the words to the pictures.

squat

squint

squid

squirrel

square

squirt

Learning Tip: Point out to your child that the **squ blend** is a combination of the **s sound** and the **qu blend**. Ensure they can say **qu** before adding the **s sound** in front of it.

The THR Blend

Say the words, and trace the **thr**'s.
Then draw lines to match the words to the pictures.

thread

three

throw

throat

thrill

throne

Learning Tip: The **thr blend** is a combination of two sounds, not three.
It is a blend of the two-letter **unvoiced th sound** with the **r sound**.

The SHR Blend

Say the words, and trace the **shr**'s.
Then draw lines to match the words to the pictures.

shrimp

shrug

shrew

shrub

shrink

shred

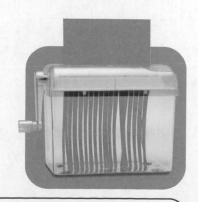

Learning Tip: The **shr blend** is a combination of two sounds, not three.
It is a blend of the two-letter **sh sound** and the **r sound**.

Three-Letter S Blends

Say each word and listen for the **s blend**. Then trace the letters, and draw lines to match the words to the pictures.

strong

scream

spring

splash

stripes

screw

Learning Tip: The **s blends** on this page are made up of **three letters** and **three sounds**. Sound out the words so your child can hear all three sounds in the blend.

More S Blends

Say the words and listen for the **s blends**.
Then draw lines to match the words with the same **s blend**.

scratch

spray

splat

string

screen

stretch

sprint

splits

Learning Tip: To identify each blend, your child will need to listen to all three letter sounds. If your child finds this hard, say the word slowly, stretching out the sounds.

Two-Letter Blends

Sound out each side of the problem. Then blend the sounds to make one word. Write the word.

 **fl + ag = _f_ _l_ _a_ _g_**

 **st + op = _ _ _ _**

 **tw + in = _ _ _ _**

 **fr + og = _ _ _ _**

 **sk + ip = _ _ _ _**

Learning Tip: If your child hasn't learned about the plus sign and addition yet, tell them that the plus sign means you put the two parts together to make one word.

Three-Letter Blends

Sound out each side of the problem. Then blend the sounds to make one word. Draw a line to match the problem with its answer.

scr + ub = •

str + um =

squ + ish =

spl + ash =

spr + out =

Learning Tip: Talk about how some of these words are onomatopoeic (they sound like their meaning). E.g., *squish*, *splash*, and *strum*. Others include *squeak* and *spring*.

The Schwa Sound

When talking, we often use an **uh** (or **ih**) **sound** instead of another vowel sound. This is called the **schwa sound**. Say the words and listen for the **uh sound**. Then trace the **a**'s.

agree

afraid

asleep

awake

alarm

America

Learning Tip: Although it is not always recognized as a true sound in English, the **schwa sound** is the most common sound of all.

The Lazy Schwa

Trace each line to match the picture with the word.
Then say the word and listen for an **uh** or **ih schwa sound**.
Trace the letter that stands for the **schwa sound**.

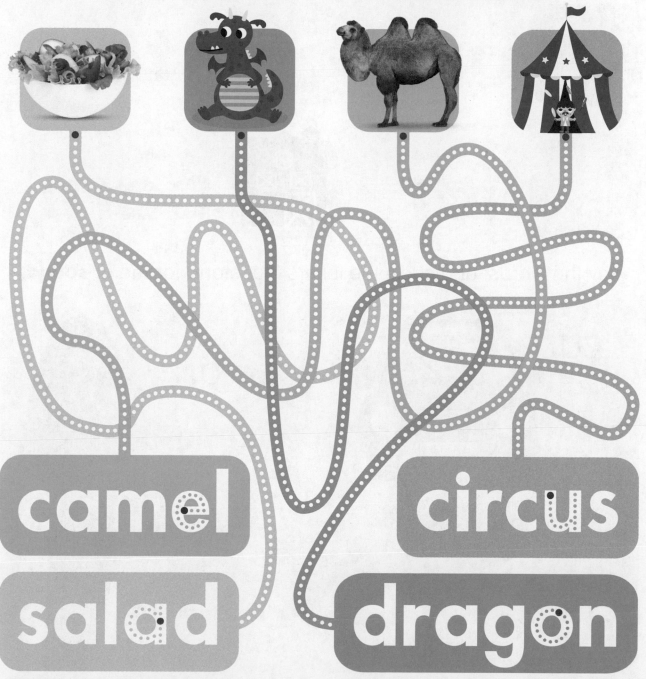

camel

circus

salad

dragon

Learning Tip: The **schwa sound** is often made in place of the vowel sound in unstressed syllables. Say words as they're said in everyday speech to hear the **schwa sound**.

The AR Sound

Say the words and listen for the **ar sound**.
Then trace the letters that stand for the **ar sound**.

arm star

jar barn

Say the words, and circle the letters that stand for the **ar sound**.

car

art

shark

Learning Tip: When the letter **r** follows a vowel, it changes the vowel's sound. Words with this letter pattern are called **r-controlled vowels**.

Listen for AR

Say the words and listen for the **ar sound**.
Trace the letters that stand for the **ar sound**.
Then draw lines to match the words to the pictures.

harp

cart

yarn

card

bark

scarf

Woof!

Learning Tip: If your child finds the **r-controlled sound** difficult to hear, say the words *cat* and *cart* several times together, and listen to how the vowel sound changes.

Find the AR Sound

Sound out the words and listen for the **ar sound**.
Circle the word in each pair that has the **ar sound**.

had	hard
march	munch
park	pack
party	pans
damp	dark
pant	part
far	for
scar	scan

Learning Tip: While the letters **ar** often stand for the **ar sound**, other letters can also stand for the same sound. E.g., *father* and *calm*.

AR Sound Art

Say the sentence and listen for the **ar sound**.
Then circle 6 **ar**'s, and finish coloring the picture.

Farmer Bart has a large barn in his farmyard.

Learning Tip: Centuries ago, the **r** in **r-controlled vowels** was sounded like an **initial r**. It is rarely heard these days.

The UR Sound

Say the words and listen for the **ur sound**.
Then trace the letters that stand for the **ur sound**.

 surf    bird

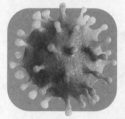 germ    stir

Say the words, and circle the letters that stand for the **ur sound**.

desserts

girl   turtle

Learning Tip: The **ur sound** can be spelled in different ways.
The most common ways are **ur**, **ir**, and **er**.

Listen for UR

Say the words and listen for the **ur sound**.
Trace the letters that stand for the **ur sound**.
Then draw lines to match the words to the pictures.

nurse

shirt

person

third

purple

circle

Learning Tip: Depending on pronunciation, the **er** at the end of words such as *sister*, *river*, and *under* can stand for the **ur sound** or the **schwa sound** (see page 204).

UR Sound Art

Say the sentence and listen for the **ur sound**. Then circle the letters that stand for 4 **ur sounds**. They are spelled **ur** and **ir**.

Kurt's first birthday is on Thursday.

Learning Tip: Encourage your child to find the **ur sounds** by listening to the words first. If necessary, remind them of the two spellings of the sound in the sentence.

Find the UR Sound

Sound out the words and listen for the **ur sound**.
Circle the word in each pair that has the **ur sound**.

skit	skirt
burn	bun
perch	pinch
turtle	tattle
prune	purse
three	thirty
torn	turn
fir	for

Learning Tip: Other less common letter combinations can also stand for the **ur sound** (e.g., *ear*n, *wor*k, and *myrrh*), but they are not taught here.

The OR Sound

Say the words and listen for the **or sound**.
Then trace the letters that stand for the **or sound**.

horn   saw

corn   paw

Say the words, and circle the letters that stand for the **or sound**.

horse   crawl   yawn   core

Learning Tip: The **or sound** can be spelled in different ways.
This page introduces two of the most common ways: **or** and **aw**.

Listen for OR

Say the words and listen for the **or sound**.
Trace the letters that stand for the **or sound**.
Then draw lines to match the words to the pictures.

orca

walk

fall

wall

talk

straw

Learning Tip: This page introduces the **a** spelling of the **or sound**.
It usually occurs in front of either **ll** (e.g., *wall*) or **lk** (e.g., *walk*).

OR Sound Art

Say the sentence and listen for the **or sound**. Then circle the letters that stand for 5 **or sounds**. They are spelled **au**, **aw**, **a**, and **or**.

Paul saw a small horse in a stall.

Learning Tip: Encourage your child to find the **or sounds** by listening to the words first. If necessary, remind them of the four spellings of the **or sound** in the sentence.

Find the OR Sound

Sound out the words and listen for the **or sound**.
Circle the word in each pair that has the **or sound**.

part	port
hunt	haul
short	shirt
boom	born
haunt	hunt
draw	drop
on	or
alive	all

Learning Tip: Other less common letter combinations can also stand for the **or sound** (e.g., *dinosaur*, *pour*, *broad*, *door*, and *caught*), but they are not taught here.

The AIR Sound

Say the words and listen for the **air sound**.
Then trace the letters that stand for the **air sound**.

hair   pair

hare   pear

Say the words, and circle the letters that stand for the **air sound**.

square

chair   bear

Learning Tip: Discuss the three most common spellings for the **air sound** (*air*, *are*, and *ear*) with your child. Ask them to find words above with the same spelling.

Listen for AIR

Say the words and listen for the **air sound**.
Trace the letters that stand for the **air sound**.
Then draw lines to match the words to the pictures.

stairs

share

stare

fairy

bare

wear

Learning Tip: If your child has difficulty reading the words, remind them that the dotted tracing letters stand for the **air sound**.

AIR Sound Art

Say the sentence and listen for the **air sound**. Then circle the letters that stand for 5 **air sounds**. They are spelled **eir**, **ear**, **are**, and **air**.

Their hairy bear gave Clare a scare.

Learning Tip: This sentence introduces a new **air sound** spelling: *their*. Encourage your child to find the **air sounds** by listening to the words first.

Find the AIR Sound

Sound out the words and listen for the **air sound**.
Circle the word in each pair that has the **air sound**.

where	when
fare	farm
care	came
them	there
sport	spare
dart	dare
part	pair
air	art

Learning Tip: This page introduces the **ere** spelling of the **air sound**. Other less common letter combinations can also stand for the **air sound**. E.g., million*aire*, pr*ayer*.

R-Controlled Vowels

Say the word for each picture. Then draw a line
to show whether it has the **ar**, **ur**, **or**, or **air sound**.

bird

car

turkey

bear

ar

ur

or

air

stork

fork

shark

fern

fairy

Learning Tip: When the letter **r** follows one or more vowels, it changes their pronunciation
from their usual short vowel sound. *Turkey*, *fern*, and *bird* all have the **ur sound**.

Listen and Match

Say the words and listen for the **vowel sounds**.
Trace the letters that stand for **vowel sounds** you have just learned.
Then draw lines to match the words to the pictures.

annoy

chair

skirt

marble

hurt

fawn

Learning Tip: The **vowel sounds** represented by the tracing letters
in the words above are taught on pages 204–221.

Word Search

Say each word and listen to the **vowel sounds**.
Then find and circle the words in the word search.

awake · small · cart · asleep · horse · large

square · hair · circle · tall · curly · short

h	a	i	r	b	g	c	a	r	t
m	p	o	w	s	h	o	r	t	i
i	h	v	a	s	l	e	e	p	k
f	o	t	w	r	a	o	j	z	c
s	r	c	a	o	r	i	c	g	u
q	s	i	k	p	g	n	d	e	r
u	e	r	e	h	e	t	a	l	l
a	o	c	c	e	w	t	a	l	y
r	d	l	a	r	g	e	o	h	b
e	x	e	c	a	s	m	a	l	l

Learning Tip: For an extra activity, pair the words first by meaning
(e.g., *small* and *large*) and then by vowel sound (e.g., *cart* and *large*).

Find the Rhyme

Say the words and listen to the **middle** and **end sounds**.
Then draw lines to match the words that **rhyme**.

pork

squirt

blister

purse

whirl

sister

shirt

twirl

star

fork

care

car

nurse

bear

Learning Tip: If needed, help your child notice that while *shirt*, *squirt*, *swirl*, and *twirl* all have the **ur sound**, they form two different rhyming pairs.

The OI Sound

Say the words and listen for the **oi sound**.
Then trace the letters that stand for the **oi sound**.

5 coin   TOYS toys

boy   Oink! oink

Say the words, and circle the letters that stand for the **oi sound**.

join

point   toilet   joy

Learning Tip: The most common spellings of the **oi sound** are **oi** and **oy**.
Two vowel sounds glide together to create a sound known as a **diphthong**.

Listen for OI

Say the words and listen for the **oi sound**.
Trace the letters that stand for the **oi sound**.
Then draw lines to match the words to the pictures.

oil

soil

coil

royal

noise

oyster

Learning Tip: While words like *tortoise* and *porpoise* contain the letters **oi**, the sound is unstressed, and we often pronounce the letters as the **schwa sound** (see page 204).

227

Find the OI Sound

Sound out the words and listen for the **oi sound**.
Circle the word in each pair that has the **oi sound**.

annoy	apple
toybox	tomato
enemy	enjoy
poison	pond
spoil	spot
boat	boil
foil	fill
coy	cot

Learning Tip: For extra practice, discuss which sounds the two words in a pair have in common and which sounds are different.

OI Sound Art

Say the sentence and listen for the **oi sound**. Then circle the letters that stand for 5 **oi sounds**. They are spelled **oi** and **oy**.

Roy is a boy who enjoys noisy toys.

Learning Tip: The **oy** spelling of the **oi sound** most often comes at the **end** of a word, while the **oi** spelling usually comes at the **start** or in the **middle** of a word.

The OU Sound

Say the words and listen for the **ou sound**.
Then trace the letters that stand for the **ou sound**.

out   cow

owl   loud

Say the words, and circle the letters that stand for the **ou sound**.

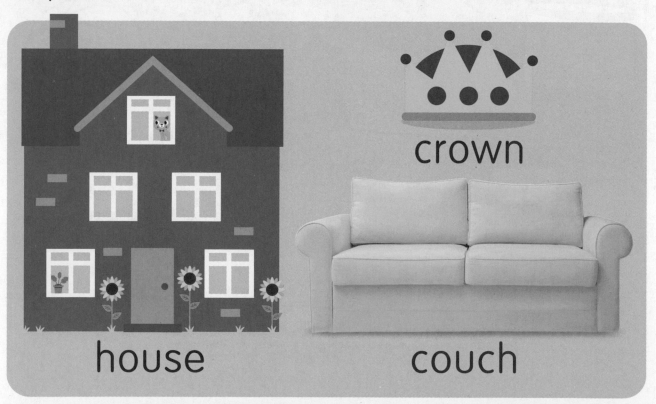

crown

house   couch

Learning Tip: Like the oi sound, the **ou sound** is a **diphthong**.
Two vowel sounds glide together to create one sound.

Listen for OU

Say the words and listen for the **ou sound**.
Trace the letters that stand for the **ou sound**.
Then draw lines to match the words to the pictures.

mouse

flower

wow

brown

cloud

mouth

Learning Tip: Most words that **end** with the **ou sound** have the **ow spelling**, while both **ou** and, less often, **ow** appear in the **middle** of words.

231

Find the OU Sound

Sound out the words and listen for the **ou sound**.
Circle the word in each pair that has the **ou sound**.

down	duck
socks	sound
frill	frown
proud	price
town	tug
bound	bundle
ouch	such
hot	how

Learning Tip: If your child finds this difficult, ask them to figure out if a word has the letters **ou** or **ow**, and if it does, to sound out the word using the **ou sound**.

OU Sound Art

Say the sentence and listen for the **ou sound**. Then circle the letters that stand for 4 **ou sounds**. They are spelled **ou** and **ow**.

A proud mouse buys a brown gown.

Learning Tip: Other less common letter combinations can also stand for the **ou sound** (e.g., **hou**r and dr**ough**t), but they are not taught here.

The Long OO Sound

Say the words and listen for the **long oo sound**.
Then trace the letters that stand for the **long oo sound**.

zoo   ruby

chew   blue

Say the words, and circle the letters that stand for the **long oo sound**.

moose   broom   screw

spooky

Learning Tip: Four common spellings of the **long oo sound** are taught here.
They are **oo** (*hoot*), **ue** (*clue*), **ew** (*drew*), and **u** (*July*).

Listen for Long oo

Say the words and listen for the **long oo sound**.
Trace the letters that stand for the **long oo sound**.
Then draw lines to match the words to the pictures.

balloon

flew

tooth

ruler

jewel

glue

Learning Tip: In America, the **long oo sound** is often heard in words such as *tube* and *new*. Elsewhere, the **long u sound** (as in *cube*) is heard in these vowords.

The Short OO Sound

Say the words and listen for the **short oo sound**.
Then trace the letters that stand for the **short oo sound**.

book   hood

foot   push

Say the words, and circle the letters that stand for the **short oo sound**.

cookie   goodbye   hook

pull

Learning Tip: Two of the most common spellings of the **short oo sound** are taught here. They are **oo** (*cook*) and **u** (*put*).

Short OO Sound Art

Say the sentence and listen for the **short oo sound**. Then circle the letters that stand for 6 **short oo sounds**. They have the **oo** spelling.

Brooke took a good book to the book nook.

Learning Tip: Other less common letter combinations can also stand for the **short oo sound** (e.g., *would* and *wolf*), but they are not taught here.

Is It OI or OU?

Say the word for each picture. Does it have the **oi sound** or the **ou sound**? Draw lines to match the words with the correct sound.

cow

toy

shout

soy

boy

oi

ou

howl

plow

house

Learning Tip: If your child finds this activity difficult, look back at the activities on pages 226–233 to review the sounds and the spellings that stand for them.

Long or Short OO?

Say each word. If it has a **long oo sound**, circle it in **green**.
If it has a **short oo sound**, circle it in **red**.

boots

woof

Woof!

look

goose

moon

hook

bush

wool

grew

flute

Learning Tip: If your child doesn't know which **oo sound** to use when sounding out a new word, suggest they try both and listen to which one sounds right.

Double Consonants

Read each word aloud, only sounding out the **double letters** once.
Trace the **double letters**, and match the words to the pictures.

drill

cliff

off

buzz

sniff

kiss

Learning Tip: The FLOSS spelling rule tells us to double the last letter for a one-syllable word that ends in **f**, **l**, **s**, or **z**. (Exceptions include *his*, *yes*, *us*, and *this*.)

Double L

Sound out each word. Only say the **l sound** once. Trace the **double l**'s. Then draw lines to match the words to the pictures.

bell

ill

shell

gull

well

spill

> **Learning Tip:** For extra practice, ask your child to find two words that rhyme with *bell* and one word that rhymes with *ill*.

Middle Doubles

The vowel in front of **double letters** has a **short vowel sound**.
Say the words and listen for the **short vowel sound** in the
first syllable. Then circle the **double letters**.

skipping

egg

puppy

carrot

hippo

pillow

dinner

muffin

bottle

Learning Tip: If your child is ready, help them notice that while the **first vowel** in these
words has a **short vowel sound**, the second vowel can have a short or long sound.

Double Spellings

Say the word for each picture and notice if the first vowel has a **long** or **short vowel sound**. Then circle the correct spelling. It will have a **double letter**.

 (**rabbit**) / rabit

 juggle / jugle

 buterfly / butterfly

 hopping / hoping

 apple / aple

 parot / parrot

 mitens / mittens

zipper / ziper

 leter / letter

 buton / button

Learning Tip: Without the double letter, the **first vowel** in many words changes to a **long vowel**. Compare these pairs: *dinner/diner, tapped/taped, mopping/moping.*

243

Ending S Blends

Say the word for each picture and listen for the **s blend** at the **end**.
Then draw a line to the letters that stand for that **blend**.

desk

sp

ghost

nest

sk

wasp

mask

st

toast

Learning Tip: This section focuses on **consonant blends** at the **end** of words.
Help your child notice both the **s sound** and the **other sound** in each blend.

Find S Blends

Sound out the words and listen for the **s blends** at the **end**.
Then draw lines to match each word with its rhyming partner.

just   crisp   best

disk   test   must   risk   lisp

Read the sentences and listen for **s blends**. Circle the letters that stand for 3 **ending s blends** and 1 **middle s blend**.

We like crisp toast.
It tastes the best!

Learning Tip: It is harder to hear blends that aren't at the start of a word. Your child may need to hear the words several times to identify the **ending** and **middle s blends**.

245

Ending L Blends

Say the word for each picture and listen for the **l blend** at the **end**.
Then draw a line to the letters that stand for that **blend**.

melt

belt

ld

lf

wolf

lk

child

lp

sulk

lt

help

Learning Tip: Help your child hear the blend by saying the word slowly, exaggerating each letter sound. Then run the last two sounds together to create the consonant blend.

Find L Blends

Say the words and listen for the **l blends** at the **end**.
Then draw lines to match each word with its rhyming partner.

cold   elf   bolt   milk

colt

silk   old   shelf

Read the sentence and listen for **l blends**. Circle the letters that
stand for 4 **ending l blends** and 1 **middle l blend**.

A child helped Alf feed the wild colt.

Learning Tip: If your child is finding this difficult, help them say each word slowly
to first identify the **l sound** and then the **l blend**.

Extra Ending Blends

Say the word for each picture and listen for the **ending blend**.
Then draw a line to the letters that stand for that **blend**.

hand

mp

wink

nt

tent

ant

nk

jump

nd

chimp

Learning Tip: The **nk sound** is first introduced on page 134. If necessary, remind your child that it is a blend of the **ng sound** and the **k sound**.

Find Ending Blends

Sound out the words and listen for the **ending blends**. Then draw lines to match each word with its rhyming partner.

kind   stamp   sent

band   mind

lamp   went   land

Read the sentence and listen for **ending blends**. Circle the letters that stand for 4 **ending blends** and 1 **middle blend**.

The elephant dunked his trunk and took a drink.

Learning Tip: Remind your child that two consonants together can stand for one sound (e.g., *elephant*) or for a blend of two sounds (e.g., *elephant*).

More Ending Blends

Say the word for each picture and listen for the **ending blend**.
Then draw a line to the letters that stand for that **blend**.

bird

ct

Woof!

bark

fork

ft

card

raft

rd

rk

insect

Learning Tip: Words ending in **rd** and **rk** often have **r-controlled vowels**.
The **r** changes the sound of the vowel in front of it (see pages 206–221).

Find Ending Blends

Sound out the words and listen for the **ending blends**. Then draw lines to match each word with its rhyming partner.

fact   yard   loft

soft   park

dark   act   hard

Read the sentence and listen for **blends**. Circle the letters that stand for 5 **blends** that are followed by **s**.

Larks, swifts, and storks are birds that eat insects.

Learning Tip: For extra practice, ask your child to find two beginning consonant blends in the first line. (They are **sw** and **st**. See pages 190–193).

Ending Blends

Say the word for each picture and listen for the **ending blend**.
Then use the words below to help you fill in the missing letters.

sink   plant   bald   blond   gift

| b | a | | |

| g | i | | |

| s | i | | |

| b | l | o | |

| p | l | a | |

Learning Tip: For extra practice, ask your child to find two beginning consonant blends in these words. (They are **bl** and **pl**. See pages 186–189).

Middle Blends

Say each word aloud and listen for the **middle blend**.
Then draw lines to match the words to the pictures.

rooster

sharks

folded

stinky

painting

Learning Tip: These middle blends are represented by the same letters as ending blends. Each one's root word has the letter blend at the end (e.g., *paint/painting*).

Practice Long A

Say the words and listen for the **long a sound**.
Then trace the letters that stand for the **long a sound**.

apron

whale

crayons

maid

shake

chain

Learning Tip: This activity reviews spelling patterns that stand for the **long a sound**.
These were introduced on pages 138–141.

Long A or Short A?

Say the words. Circle the words with the **long a sound** in **green**.
Circle the words with the **short a sound** in **red**.

flame

van

stamp

acorn

sailor

braids

hand

space

clap

plane

anchor

acrobat

Learning Tip: If your child finds this difficult, discuss the spelling patterns that stand for the **long a sound** on page 254, and ask them to look for them here.

Just A

Sometimes, an **a** on its own stands for the **long a sound**. Write the missing **a** in each word. Then say the word with a **long a sound**.

b_con

b_by

r_dio

t_ble

l_dy

p_per

D_vid

_ngel

Learning Tip: Some words are spelled in ways that don't conform to usual pronunciation patterns. Let your child know this and practice the words with them.

Hard Long A Words

Read the words aloud. Say the **long a sound** where you see **dark letters**. Then draw lines to match the words to the pictures.

veil

steak

obey

eight

neigh

reindeer

Neigh!

8

Learning Tip: This page introduces some uncommon ways of spelling the **long a sound**. Other even less common spellings (e.g., *gauge*, *suede*, *beret*) are not taught here.

Practice Long E

Say the words and listen for the **long e sound**.
Then trace the letters that stand for the **long e sound**.

peach

muddy

candy

Cheep!

cheep

cheese

reach

Learning Tip: This activity reviews spelling patterns that stand for the **long e sound**.
These were introduced on pages 142–145.

Long E or Short E?

Say the words. Circle the words with the **long e sound** in **blue**. Circle the words with the **short e sound** in **orange**.

teeth

puppy

egg

yes

net

see

smell

scream

press

vest

forty

leash

Learning Tip: If your child finds this difficult, discuss the spelling patterns that stand for the **long e sound** on page 258, and ask them to look for them here.

Other Long E Words

In some words, an **e** on its own stands for the **long e sound**.
Trace the **e** in each word. Then say the word with a **long e sound**.

me   **we**

he   **she**   **be**

Sound out the words. When you see the letters **ie**,
make the **long e sound**. Then trace the **ie**'s.

berries   **puppies**

lilies   **cookie**

Learning Tip: If your child is ready for it, discuss how some of the words above
are the plural of words that end in **y** (*lily, berry, puppy*).

Hard Long E Words

Read the words aloud. Say the **long e sound** where you see **dark letters**. Then draw lines to match the words to the pictures.

key

people

honey

monkey

turkey

machine

Learning Tip: This page introduces some uncommon ways of spelling the **long e sound**. Other even less common spellings (e.g., *debris*, *deceive*, *esprit*) are not taught here.

Practice Long I

Read the sentences aloud and listen for the **long i sound**.
Then trace the letters that stand for the **long i sound**.

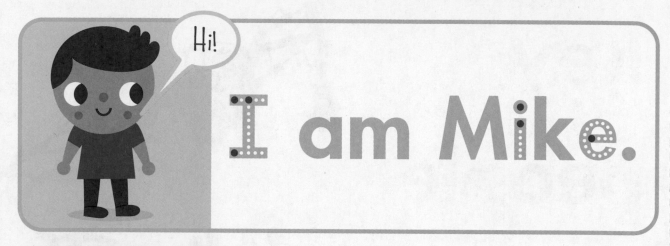

I am Mike.

I ride my bike.

I fly my kite.

Learning Tip: This activity reviews spelling patterns that stand for the **long i sound**. These were introduced on pages 146–149.

Long I or Short I?

Say the words. Circle the words with the **long i sound** in **red**.
Circle the words with the **short i sound** in **blue**.

cry

slime

6 six

lion

drive

chick

spy

swim

kick

gift

THIS WAY! sign

sprint

Learning Tip: If your child finds this difficult, discuss the spelling patterns that stand
for the **long i sound** on page 262, and ask them to look for them here.

Other Long I Sounds

Sound out the words. Where you see **ie** or **igh**, make the **long i sound**. Then trace the letters that stand for the **long i sound**.

pie

high

tie

light

fries

fright

knight

died

Learning Tip: So far, this book has covered five ways of making the **long i sound**: i (*idea*), i_e (*wise*), y (*July*), ie (*lie*), and igh (*right*).

Hard Long I Words

Say these words and listen for the **long i sound**.
Then trace the letters that stand for the **long i sound**.

eye   bye

buy   kayak

Say the sentence and listen for 4 **long i sounds**.
Circle the letters that stand for the **long i sound**.

I spy with my little eye.

Learning Tip: This page introduces some uncommon ways of spelling the **long i sound**.
Other even less common spellings (e.g., *aisle*, *height*) are not taught here.

265

Practice Long 0

Say the words and listen for the **long o sound**.
Then trace the letters that stand for the **long o sound**.

piano

pose

throw

goat

toast

hello

Learning Tip: This activity reviews spelling patterns that stand for the **long o sound**. These were introduced on pages 150–153.

Long O or Short O?

Say the words. Circle the words with the **long o sound** in **green**. Circle the words with the **short o sound** in **blue**.

no

sock

bone

fox

knock

box

float

stop

robe

throne

crow

frog

Learning Tip: If your child finds this difficult, discuss the spelling patterns that stand for the **long o sound** on page 266, and ask them to look for them here.

The OE Spelling

Sound out the words. Where you see the letters **oe** say the **long o sound**. Then trace the **oe**'s, and draw lines to match the words with the pictures.

toes

hoe

doe

Joe

oboe

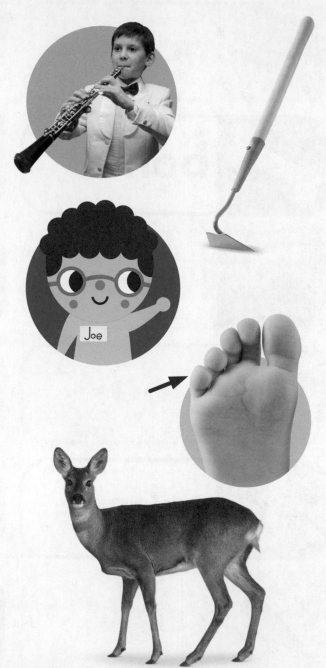

Joe

Learning Tip: So far, this book has covered five ways of making the **long o sound**: **o** (*ocean*), **o_e** (*joke*), **oa** (*road*), **ow** (*grow*), and **oe** (*goes*).

Hard Long O Words

Say these words and listen for the **long o sound**.
Then trace the letters that stand for the **long o sound**.

sew   Oh!   yolk

Say the sentence and listen for 3 **long o sounds**.
Circle the letters that stand for the **long o sound**.

A goat ate Milo's coat!

Learning Tip: This page introduces some uncommon ways of spelling the **long o sound**.
Other even less common spellings (e.g., *though*, *brooch*, *depot*) are not taught here.

Practice Long U

Say the words and listen for the **long u sound**.
Then trace the letters that stand for the **long u sound**.

unicorn

Mew!

mew

huge

music

mute

universe

Learning Tip: This activity reviews spelling patterns that stand for the **long u sound**. These were introduced on pages 154–157.

Long U or Short U?

Say the words. Circle the words with the **long u sound** in **green**.
Circle the words with the **short u sound** in **red**.

cube

gum

drum

pew

rush

human

uniform

duck

slug

museum

skunk

unicycle

Learning Tip: If your child finds this difficult, discuss the spelling patterns that stand for the **long u sound** on page 270, and ask them to look for them here.

Hard Long U Words

Say the words and listen for the **long u sound**.
Then trace the letters that stand for the **long u sound**.

 you  view  ewe

Say the sentence and listen for 3 **long u sounds**.
Circle the letters that stand for the **long u sound**.

ZOO

I see a few cute emus.

Learning Tip: This page introduces some uncommon ways of spelling the **long u sound**. Other even less common spellings (e.g., *debut*, *feud*) are not taught here.

Long Vowels

Say these words with **long vowel sounds**.
Then draw lines to match the words with their **rhyming partners**.

maybe **eight**

so **write**

plate **pea**

few

we

baby

night

low

rise

mew **skies**

Learning Tip: The **rhyming part** of each word on this page contains
a **long vowel sound**. Help your child to identify it.

Which Vowel Sound?

Say the word for the picture. Then check the right vowel sound.

long **a** ✓
short **a** ☐

long **o** ☐
long **e** ☐

long **i** ☐
long **e** ☐

long **u** ☐
short **u** ☐

short **o** ☐
long **o** ☐

long **a** ☐
short **a** ☐

long **i** ☐
short **i** ☐

long **e** ☐
short **e** ☐

long **i** ☐
short **i** ☐

short **u** ☐
short **o** ☐

Learning Tip: For extra practice, ask your child to say each word using the incorrect vowel sound and laugh together at how it sounds.

Phonics Art

Sound out each word. Then use the key to color that part of the picture.

Vowel Sound Key

long a = blue, **long e = red**, long i = green, long o = orange,
long u = pink, short a = yellow, **short e = purple**,
short i = brown, **short o = black**, short u = gray

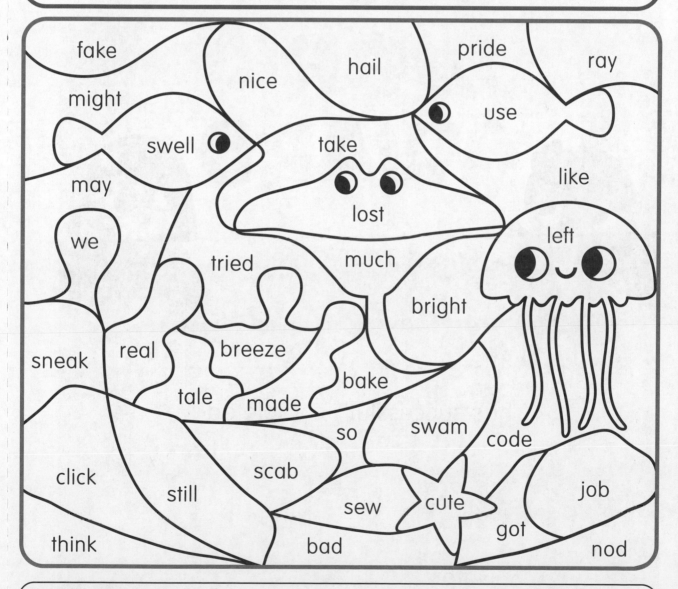

Learning Tip: Talk about the words together, and ask your child why they think a word has a particular vowel sound. Help them remember rules and compare similar words.

Congratulations!

GREAT WORK AWARD

Name: ....

has successfully completed

GIANT PHONICS

Date: ....